"This guy who I interviewe
woman than practically an
He truly is the real deal."

MW00583198

~ David DeAngelo, doubleyourdating.com

"I read your book 'Secrets of Female Sexuality' and I can't thank you enough for the valuable information. It just blew me away... finally someone understood me.

"I truly believe this book is the key to a successful loving partnership. If everyone out there would read this book, all the therapists would go out of business; no one would need them anymore.

This should be a mandatory read for both Women and the Men we so dearly love and appreciate when they are being MEN and allowing us to be WOMEN!"

~ Jean R, Maryland

"I started reading your book 'The Secrets Of Female Sexuality' and I had to continue until I finished it. You are right on the money!!! The 4 things a woman wants is so true. When someone asks what I am looking for, I tell them just that.

"The problem is, the majority of men think they are giving you that and they are sooooo far off.

I am definitely going to recommend this book to my male friends as well as my female friends.

"The reasons you describe why a woman goes outside her marriage really hit home. They are all so true.

"I truly believe every guy who seriously wants to have a great relationship with a woman read this material. All 3 of your books are very well written, and should be recommended to anyone who is interested in a fulfilling relationship. Heck, all men should be

'required' to read this stuff. Sex therapists should be sharing your name with their clients. Had any of my partners had this information years ago, my life sure would have turned out differently!!

This stuff is awesome! You did a wonderful job at putting this together and I will definitely spread the word!! Thanks!! Keep up the great work!!"

~ Cindy Moore, Michigan

"As a woman I think that in fact what you are doing is a public service for women everywhere."

~ Val, Orange County California

"David, all bookstores in the United States should throw away every book on sexuality for straight men and hang a sign with a link to your website. No man will ever need anything else."

~ Jay, Boston Massachusetts

"Thanks David, for taking this subject out of the garb of mystery and teaching it to normal guys to help them on the road to fulfillment in their lives."

~ Scott M., Ireland

"I say again, you are the voice in the wilderness and the best source of information and encouragement for us guys who enjoy giving women incredible orgasms.

Keep up the great work."

~Jim G., Georgia

"This is one rare book that indeed delivers on its premise and doesn't disappoint. This 'Brutally Honest Truth' about female sexuality is still a 'secret' to most people, men and women alike, probably because it is an uncomfortable truth to admit. Yet, I wouldn't be surprised if this ignorance is at the root of most relationship issues."

~Stephane Chiche, New York

"This is the most important book I've ever read. I say this because the greatest pain in my life has come from sexual rejection and, worse, not knowing why a woman I loved dumped me for a bad boy who treated her like garbage. I was convinced that my tragic flaws were that I was intelligent, sensitive and respectful of woman. What David Shade does is describe the problem and, better, offers the solution. I have learned why women have rejected me and I have learned that what I thought were my weaknesses are actually my strengths. I can use my intelligence to turn a woman on with my words and I can use my sensitivity to observe her carefully.

"After I read this book I underwent a transformation of my consciousness that was so profound, it exhausted me and I had to spend a weekend sleeping to recover. And the strange thing is when I did go out I ran into two beautiful women I had desired and they both approached me where before they kept their distance. I feel that David Shade is a pioneer in the sense that he had the courage to travel into a very dark and mysterious forest of female sexuality and emerge with a story to tell that is inspiration and healing. David Shade is the Shaman of Sexuality."

~Sean Heffernan, Colorado

"This is the best material out there anywhere for anyone who wants to understand female sexuality and how to help a high self esteem woman discover and experience her innate feminine self. I'm a long time student of this topic including a Ph.D. in a closely related area if that gives my opinion any credibility. David is right

on the mark with his philosophy about how to establish an unbelievably intimate and fulfilling relationship between a caring man who values, respects and appreciates women for the wonderful creatures that they are and a woman who believes she is entitled to enjoy her body for the incredible pleasure of which she is capable."

~Dr. Greene, Georgia

"This book tells it like it is. It's frank, startlingly so at times, and can be just what the doctor ordered to break you free from the way your parents / your friends / society at large tells you how you should be doing things. For some people it'll require no small measure of courage, both to accept that what they're currently doing isn't good enough and to do what's necessary to build the amazing sex life they desire and deserve. I think it's worth it, and I think this book holds the key."

~Rick & Lysa, Canada

"Women BEG for men to know and practice the information Shade has been teaching and writing. Not only is this book incredible, ALL of his material is just as powerful. Google 'David Shade' and get the rest of his materials. Sign up for his newsletters if you're skeptical. Not only is his material helpful as a 'lover', it's also very helpful to become the BEST man 'EVERY WOMAN WANTS'. Women have NO idea how much sexual potential she has, until she has met a MAN that has been taught by 'The Masterful-Lover' himself. Give your girlfriend the wonderful and beautiful gift of feeling like a truly sexual woman. You'll be the man she's always dreamed of being with, I PROMISE."

~Z. Libby, Michigan

"My first experience with David Shade was with one of his earliest products, 'The Manual'. Before reading it, I always thought I was getting GOOD advice from my buddies, other sex books, magazines, and movies; after reading his stuff, it was clear just how misdirected I was.

"I now get a huge chuckle out of seeing how misinformed, ignorant, and often just plain backwards the rest of the world of sex advice is compared to David Shade's material.

"My own personal success with women in bed improved dramatically after reading this book. Women started complimenting me, and I gained the confidence that can only come from knowing you CAN rock a woman's world in bed. Quote from one of my girlfriends: 'You know my body better than I do myself.'

"David Shade is the real deal. You can consider his material thoroughly vetted and utterly devoid of self-promotion, self-aggrandizement, misogyny, and other B.S.- he really can back up what he says with real-world experience and examples.

"If you really want to give women incredible pleasure, I can't think of a faster or better route there than buying a David Shade book."
~Robert, Seattle Washington

"David has Really scored here! Even better you will have really scored if you get this book!

"This book will turn on its head your total conception of what you think women want in the bedroom...and outside. More importantly it will turn your sex life into the one you have always fantasized about.

If you are a little weak in the knees about sexual talk... then you might pass on this book, but if you are ready to have women looking at you as if you are a superstar... in the bedroom and out, you must get this book now.

Start improving your love life and the love life of women. I think women should read this book and buy copies for the men in their lives. Like David said "They all wish you knew... but won't tell you." But here is what he didn't tell you... Once you treat a woman like this 'They will tell you!' They will tell you in ways that you have always dreamed of being told by women. There is nothing better in my book than having the appreciation that a woman will give you for fully satisfying her in this way.

You are all in for a very big treat! :-)"

~Mark Ryan, New York

"I'm a man in my thirties and up until recently I bounced in and out of unsatisfying relationships (if I managed to be in a relationship at all.) As I became increasingly frustrated, I began reading books on all topics of sex and relationships. At the time, I only thought the 'sex' component of my lacking relationships was a small part, but now I know that was a wrong assumption. The things I learned reading David Shades various materials changed my life. Chances are, that won't be the case for you. But if you read this with an open mind, hold back on projecting your own beliefs into the concepts, and be willing to take risks, to think new ways and persist relentlessly, you WILL experience an amazing depth of intimacy with your partner.

Do yourself a huge favor, buy David's book. Learn about women. Learn more about yourself in the process. In doing so, you just might be rewarded with a sense of accomplishment that spills over into all aspects of your life. It happened to me."

~R. Clark, Colorado

THE SECRETS OF FEMALE SEXUALITY

BE THE MASTERFUL LOVER™ WOMEN CRAVE

DAVID SHADE

THE SECRETS OF FEMALE SEXUALITY

BE THE MASTERFUL LOVER™ WOMEN CRAVE

ISBN-13: 978-0-692-00447-0

Published by David Shade Corporation

David Shade and Masterful Lover
are registered trademarks of
David Shade Corporation

The Agreement

The information in this program is for entertainment purposes only. It is not to be taken as medical, legal, or personal advice. You assume full responsibility for the consequences of your own decisions and actions. Neither David Shade Corporation nor the author of this book will be held liable in any manner whatsoever stemming from your use of the information in this program.

You must always practice safe, protected sex. There are other books and resources from qualified medical professionals to teach you how to do that. This program assumes that you always practice safe, protected sex as directed by qualified medical professionals.

This program discusses highly controversial sexual activities. Neither David Shade Corporation nor the author of this book assume any responsibility for the exercise or misuse of the topics described herein.

There is a real and absolute distinction between explicit consensual acts between consenting adult partners for their mutual pleasure and all acts of violence against unconsenting partners. Imposing any sexual activity on a reluctant or unwilling partner (or anyone who cannot give legal consent) is a criminal offense. Further, state laws vary; some sexual activities, even between consenting adults, are illegal in certain jurisdictions.

By reading this program, you agree to the terms of this agreement. If you cannot agree to this agreement, do not read this book and immediately return this book for a full refund.

If you do agree to this agreement, then read on, play nice, give women incredible pleasure, and enjoy...

TABLE OF CONTENTS

PREFACE   XIII

SECTION ONE:
THE SECRETS

1   INTRODUCTION   2
2   MY DARKEST DAY   12
3   THE LONG ROAD TO ENLIGHTENMENT   16
4   WHAT I LEARNED FROM GIVING
     WOMEN PHONE SEX   21
5   TEN THINGS WOMEN LOVE…BUT
     WOULD NEVER ADMIT   28
6   WHAT WOMEN WANT   36
7   WOMEN'S DARK SECRET   55
8   WHY WOMEN CRAVE ROMANCE   62
9   WOMEN AND THEIR FANTASIES   64
10   WOMEN WANT MEN TO KNOW THIS   67
11   WHY WOMEN WANT TO BE LED   73
12   WHAT WOMEN ARE PISSED OFF ABOUT   84
13   DO WOMEN HAVE ALL THE POWER?   104
14   HOW WOMEN CATEGORIZE MEN   106
15   THE SECRET TO GIVING WOMEN WILD
     SCREAMING ORGASMS   116

SECTION TWO:
BE THE MASTERFUL LOVER WOMEN CRAVE

16   HOW TO BE A MASTERFUL LOVER   124
17   HOW TO UNLEASH HER INNER
     ANIMAL   155

SECTION THREE:
SUCCESS STORIES

18   THE BEST SEX I EVER HAD: MASTERFUL
     LOVER SUCCESS STORIES FROM
     AROUND THE WORLD   172

SECTION FOUR:
GUEST CHAPTERS

     INTRODUCTION FROM DAVID SHADE   214
19   MARK CUNNINGHAM   216
20   ALICIA DUNAMS   225
21   CARLOS XUMA   232
22   LENA VOYLES   244
23   BRAD P   251

SECTION FIVE:
NEXT STEPS TO BEING A MASTERFUL LOVER

     WHERE TO LEARN MORE   262
     GET YOUR FREE CD TODAY   265
     FREE VIP INNER CIRCLE OFFER   266
     FREE STUFF LINKED TO THIS BOOK   267

PREFACE

"Have you ever loved a woman until milk leaped from her as though she had just given birth to love itself and now must feed it or burst? Have you ever tasted a woman until she could believe that she could be satisfied only by consuming the tongue that had devoured her? Have you ever loved a woman so completely that the sound of your voice in her ears would cause her body to shudder and explode in such intense pleasure that only weeping could bring her full release?"
~Don Juan DeMarco

For the ladies, while I wrote this book in narrative form for other men (for obvious reasons), I want to include you, as well.

For the men, WARNING! I am going to present radical changes in your beliefs. Much of what you are about to read will be contrary and challenging to everything you have believed about female sexuality and about relationships altogether. Some men have condemned it even before reading past the first chapter. (You will read e-mails from two such men.) I have coached thousands of men, and invariably the ones who reject the truths of female sexuality are the ones who regularly find themselves alone, or worse, stuck in a very unfulfilling and unhappy marriage.

You may find that the information makes you feel uncomfortable. I went through a very painful experience as a result of misconceptions and ignorance of truths which proved to be the beginning of a journey of discovery and personal empowerment (which you will read about). Positive change is invariably accompanied by discomfort at first, but I intend to save you from the kind of pain that I went through. You have to keep an open mind.

In this book, I unapologetically present the truths of female sexuality in a brutally honest manner. Most of the other books you find in bookstores are written by 'feel good,' politically correct theorists who sell to you by telling you what you want to hear and things which are in agreement with social programming. That content is not based on real cases from the real world, and is of no help in situations where your woman is unhappy and not having orgasms (which usually go hand in hand).

I read all the books in the bookstores, and very few contained anything truly helpful. The ones that stood out were books such as "*The Hite Report*" which is 440 large pages of small print of factual reality attesting to the fact that women are unfulfilled to the point of utter madness.

I went outside the boundaries of political correctness and societal norms and tried things not done before and found the things that really work. I did the actual field work and found what women actually responded to. Nothing else matters except how women respond.

Most of what you have learned about female sexuality was probably from people who have their own misconceptions. Looking at it more closely, you will probably find that they have frustrations of their own. Unlike them, I have had success that is known worldwide. My clients have repeated these successes to give their women indescribable pleasure beyond what can be comprehended by most people. (You will read from some of them.) Hence, it is no surprise that my thesis is in contradiction to what other people may have told you before.

On another point, I suspect you may be quite skilled and successful. Most of the men who read my materials are into learning to be better lovers, and, thus, are already far ahead of most men. Many of my top clients were very impressive, yet became even more so. If you are such a man, I would like to hear from you, as we would have much to talk about.

HOW TO LEARN MORE ON
A CONTINUAL BASIS – FREE

I strive to see that the truths in this book work for you, and I hope for you to use them. In that light, I have a number of real cases from other readers, answers to questions, advice to challenges, and very useful tips in my free e-mail newsletter. To get your copy, register online at RenegadeSexExpert.com.

BOOK ROADMAP

Section One begins with a key turning point in my life, the sequence of events that began to crumble my misconceptions of sexuality, and how I began to discover the secrets. As my misconceptions were falling apart, they were replaced by my field work findings of how women actually respond. Nothing matters except how women respond. Then, by trying things that were way outside the boundaries, you will read how I made things happen that are beyond the comprehension of most people. As I outline what is really true, the secrets are fully developed and explained. I also include the key points that I learned from other authors who I respect. I then share how to apply the secrets in the noble cause of giving women wild, screaming orgasms.

Section Two is a summary of the things you must do in applying the secrets in the supreme endeavor of awakening a woman's sexuality. These are the key points. They are covered in brief so they will fit into this book and to help you to begin leveraging the secrets right away. For the interested reader, I refer you to my other works which cover the entire topic in detail, including many specific detailed examples.

Section Three includes true success stories of just a few of my clients. These serve as good examples of how to apply the secrets to make women delirious with pleasure, wildly happy, and totally loving everything about being a woman.

Section Four contains guest chapters.

Section Five is a list of resources for further discovery and development. I also included the list of books and mentors that have affected me along the way. I have consumed countless books and resources on this topic and can recommend the few that contributed leading work. This section also includes information on free offers and resources. These include a free CD, a free trial membership to the VIP Insider's Circle, and free website resources, one of which is my free e-mail course.

SECTION 1

THE SECRETS

CHAPTER 1

INTRODUCTION

"I love women."
~Hugh Hefner

First of all, let me explain that all of this information only pertains to mentally healthy women. In fact, it best fits women who are intelligent and have high self-esteem.

And when I say "women this" and "women that," I mean MOST women. Certainly, there are exceptions to everything.

This information also only applies to women who you intend to see on a continuing basis. It does not apply to one-night stands. The most important reason for this is that only women who take you seriously are going to respond to this.

Remember, when you lead a woman, you are responsible for her. As they say, "With great power comes great responsibility."

If you are familiar with my material, you know that it can at times be hard core. If you are not familiar with my material, some of it may seem a bit shocking. But let me make this perfectly clear, everything contained here is in the context of respect for women. I have the utmost respect for women. My parents raised me right.

Also, this is NOT about manipulation of women. I loathe when men try to manipulate women. Instead, this is about empowering your woman. It is about "facilitating," about "enabling."

But at the same time, I am all about results, and sometimes that takes drastic action. Let's take a very tame example.

Let's consider the case in which you are with a woman who has difficulty having orgasms...

I recommend that you do NOT tell her that the goal is for her to have an orgasm. It may be the honest truth that you want to give her an orgasm, but to tell her that is only going to make things worse, because it gives her "performance anxiety."

Therefore, it could be argued that not telling her that you intend to give her an orgasm is not telling the truth.

Well, in this case, to tell her the truth is NOT helping her.

Instead, simply tell her that you want to learn what feels good for her, tell her that you simply want her to feel the pleasure, and tell her to do exactly what you instruct her to do. Eventually, as a result, she has an orgasm!

Is that being dishonest? Is that withholding the truth? Is that manipulation?

I think that it is "facilitating" her. It has empowered her.

That was a very tame example. There will be other more powerful situations, but just because my methods are powerful and actually work, does not mean they are manipulation. My methods are "enabling."

Also, this is absolutely NOT about having power over women! Some people get that wrong.

Let's consider an e-mail from one person:

```
I was expecting something different from
this book. Please issue me a full refund.
After reading the first portion of this book
I feel like you have chosen to seek sexual
power over women to cover up the fracture of
your past. You are not yet healed. I hope
you are open and vulnerable enough to
continue seeking help, no matter how good
you are in the bedroom. Area B does not fix
the pain of area A.
```

That customer ordered the book directly from me and thus immediately received a courteous and complete refund. Still, it's too bad he didn't read the rest of the book. He would have read about the very points that he mentioned...

`"was expecting something different"`

I don't tell men what they want to hear. If he had read on, he would have read that I tell men what they need to hear.

`"seek sexual power over women"`

If he had read on, he would have learned why that is the wrong thing to do in every way. He would have learned the concept of being Personally and Sensually Powerful and the concept of empowering women.

`"cover up the fracture of the past"`

He would have read how to leverage the past to bring about an empowered future. He would have read about how I assumed responsibility for my lot in life and how I became empowered to do something about it.

`"not yet healed"`

He would have read the full story of the healing process, including the mentally healthy way to healing, based on the critical ingredient of personal responsibility, how that leads to self-empowerment, and why that builds self-esteem.

`"open and vulnerable"`

He would have read about the importance of being open and vulnerable and its magic in the context of being strong and secure. He would have understood how that integration is a truly masculine virtue and exactly why women are so drawn to it.

`"continue seeking help"`

He would have read about the importance of continuous self-improvement and how others can help. In fact, he would have read how women helped me so very much in my journey, in important and key ways they didn't know.

"no matter how good you are in the bedroom"

He would have read how being good in the bedroom is not a compensation, a cover up, or a magic pill. He missed out entirely on the resultant understanding that being good in the bedroom is merely a byproduct of all the other things.

"Area B does not fix the pain of Area A"

That is entirely congruent with my book.

I also want to say that I think that men and women are equal. I do not believe that men are superior to women. I do not believe that women are subservient to men. My parents raised me better that that.

Here is an e-mail from a man in Sweden:

I like your work and have bought all your products. I did some of it before I came across your work and I felt really good when I read your books. I understand that they are not politically correct, especially in my country (Sweden) where women and men are considered equal in every aspect, but I know you are right.

I believe that, as well. My mother has always been a woman who commanded respect and insisted on being treated equally. (Note: She was a Daddy's girl. That is a good thing.)

She and my father have always had a wonderful relationship.

They raised my sister to also command respect, which she most certainly does. (Note: She is also a Daddy's girl.)

My parents raised me to treat people with respect. They taught me that I am accountable for my own actions. I have them to thank for a loving, functional, and healthy upbringing.

But to be totally pragmatic and realistic, for the sake of a successful and exciting sexual relationship between a man and a woman, there are certain everlasting truths that must be recognized.

Women are feminine. Men are masculine.

Women like being women, and they like the contrast.

Men like being men and also like the contrast.

Part of being feminine, for most women, is to be sexually submissive.

Part of being masculine, for most men, is to lead sexually.

For the most part, women experience their sexuality in the context of the man leading.

More about this later.

Still, the question remains: is that equal?

It is not exactly "equal," it is instead "complimentary." The important thing is that it is a consensual assumption of roles in the context of mutual respect.

Interestingly, that's the situation in which most couples experience fulfilling sexual relationships.

But some people get an entirely wrong idea about *The Secrets of Female Sexuality.*" Let's consider an e-mail from another person:

> What a fool I am to get scammed again by some sleezy two-bit creep like you. For some barhopping, phone sex operating predator to think he has any idea what a "quality" woman is about is insane. Okay, so you are really good at getting in the pants of slutty, cheating women who are out looking for someone to get into their pants. Has it never occurred to you that most people are not promiscuous? The people who aren't are not spending any time at your bars or on your phone sex line. Your bullshit is not a whole lot of help to a family guy who wants to be better at loving his sweet, tender, non-cheating wife.

That person's purchase was promptly refunded, because they had ordered directly from me.

This book has absolutely nothing to do with promiscuity. This book is about the truths of female sexuality.

By the way, women are not out looking for someone to get into their pants, at least not the high-quality women. Again, all of this is only in the context of high-quality women.

When I use the term "slut," I am referring to it in a healthy way, one that describes a woman fully enjoying and celebrating her sexuality with her man and allowing herself to be ruthlessly expressive.

It does NOT refer to women who are promiscuous, seek validation from sex, or who sell themselves out. Most men are not interested in such women.

It refers to women who want to share their sexuality with their man and celebrate their sexuality and enjoy it in a ruthlessly expressive, animalistic, natural way. That's what we all really want, anyway.

And I most certainly do aim to help a family guy who wants to be better at loving his sweet, tender, non-cheating wife. I am all about that.

Here is an e-mail from such a man:

David...

I read your e-mails with interest, and was concerned enough to pen my own when I read the one from the "family guy with the non-cheating wife".

I've bought both "David Shade's Manual" and "Give Women Wild Screaming Orgasm" books, and my wife of 10 years has benefited greatly. I often surprise her with "new stuff" now, and have used the Welcomed Method and Deep Spot to take our sex life to a whole new level. She loves it!

I've benefited by no longer being so selfish in this aspect of our marriage. I now serve her, and she in turn desires to serve me more, so it's more mutual now than in the previous nine years of marriage.

And our children benefit because my wife and I are communicating better than ever and are more passionately in love.

What you've done for my marriage, David, has been amazing! You've taught me things I've never heard of before and helped make my married life far more compelling, enjoyable and fulfilling.

Dave (another family man)

Some women have been disappointed with this book. Here is a review that one very disappointed female reader left at a book marketer's website:

Had I known how repulsive, with vulgar language, this book was I would not have purchased it. The book has NO credential and seems to focus on the fantasy and imagination vs. reality...there is NO supporting research to back any of Spades claims. The stories told are border line pornographic and extremely sexist. Spade also has an annoying way of repeating his same stories and ideas throughout the book. He boasts throughout the book that his ideas work but NEVER does he give any an explanation of 'what' to do. At any rate, I found the entire book immature and repulsive with the use of vulgar language! Needless to say I just got rid of it.

Let me comment on the various comments she made. By the way, my name is Shade, not Spade, though I admire the career of comedian David Spade.

"Had I known how repulsive with vulgar language"

Truthful discussion of human sexuality must include truthful discussion of language. To do otherwise, would be to deny eroticism. If the 'f-word' makes a person uncomfortable, this book is not a good fit.

The highly respected and successful marriage counselor Dr. David Schnarch wrote in his book "*Passionate Marriage:*"

> I always experience trepidation bringing up the topic of fucking in public lecture and professional workshops. At one workshop I conducted, a woman stood up and said, "Speaking as a woman, I dislike your language! Everything in society today is f-this and f-you! I don't mind talking bout 'making love' or 'having sex', but I find the way you're talking offensive!"
>
> What could I say? I knew that anything I said would look like a defensive male authority figure discounting this woman's perspective.
>
> While I was pondering, another woman stood up. "Well, also speaking as a woman, I agree about all the dirty mouths. Everything is m-f-this and m-f-that. But I also know it's taken almost twenty years for me to get into bed with my husband and say, 'Come on, lover, fuck me good!'"

That pretty much sums it up. Now, continuing on the various comments made:

"The book has NO credential and seems to focus on the fantasy and imagination vs. reality"

The reality of female sexuality is that it has a very large component of fantasy and imagination. In fact, that is a critically important component, as is shown.

"there is NO supporting research to back any of Spades claims"

I don't know how she can say that. Numerous highly-respected pillars in the study of human sexuality have been cited.

```
"The       stories       told       are       border       line
pornographic"
```

Actual activities in the bedroom are discussed. It is truth. Calling it pornographic is just name calling.

```
"and extremely sexist"
```

Human sexuality deals with the sexes. There is no escaping that, but that does not make it sexist. Again, my parents raised me better than that. I have previously stated that everything is in the context of the utmost respect for women. Men and women are equal, but they are different, and it is the differences that make it special.

```
"Spade also has an annoying way of repeating
his same stories and ideas throughout the
book"
```

Certain critical points are illustrated in contrasting scenarios. I don't understand why that is annoying.

```
"He boasts throughout the book that his
ideas work but NEVER does he give any an
explanation of 'what' to do."
```

The 'what to do' is clearly illustrated in the examples of what worked.

```
"At any rate, I found the entire book
immature and repulsive with the use of
vulgar language! Needless to say I just got
rid of it."
```

Had she ordered it directly from me at my website, I would have happily fully refunded her for her purchase.

The fact is, many women would love to be able to tell their husband, "Come on, lover, fuck me good!" Here is an email from such a woman:

```
David,
```

Regarding that review that woman wrote. Granted, some people are language sensitive, but they need to get over it! Your material is written for men to use in the context of a successful, committed relationship. What woman would NOT want her man to express his deepest, most animalistic feelings toward her? And, she him? Your book shows men how to be just that. The strong, self confident man that his woman needs and wants. The man who will take her to heights of pleasure she only dreams and fantasizes about. I wish my now ex husband would have had this material available to him. It may well have saved our marriage.

Even Shannon Ethridge, writing to Christian women in "The Sexually Confident Wife", states that "dirty talk" is acceptable as long as both parties agree on the words being used, no matter what they are.

Cindy

With that aside, I begin with my story. I was married once...

Chapter 2

My Darkest Day

"Man's greatest motivating force
is his desire to please woman!"
~Napoleon Hill

Though it was a beautiful sunny Tuesday evening in April of 1992, it was a very dark day for me...

Returning home from work, I pulled into our subdivision of large brick homes. Golden beams of sunlight shone through the trees onto the carefully manicured lawns.

I pulled into our garage and went into the house. I hugged my two children and kissed my wife.

She was hot—a lingerie model. 5'9", 36-24-36, beautiful breasts, amazing ass, long athletic legs, long dark hair, and full red lips.

I had met her ten years before. We had sex on the third date. Two years later, we were married.

We had built a big home in the suburbs. We had two beautiful children. She and I had sex every night. It was basic vanilla sex, but we always had simultaneous orgasms. I was a happy man.

Recently, though, the frequency of sex had diminished. We had started arguing about money. It got to the point where I felt that I couldn't do anything right. I didn't know what was wrong.

I asked her to sit on the couch with me. I pleaded with her to tell me what was wrong. She simply replied, "I want a divorce, and you get the kids. I'm moving out." I was floored. I asked her to explain why, but she refused.

Later that evening, I was in my den. Behind me, was a wall full of mechanical engineering textbooks from my undergrad and electrical engineering books from my Masters degree. Before me, was a large, solid oak desk that my parents had given me for a housewarming present. They were to be the only things I would walk away with after the divorce.

I picked up the phone to make a call. I heard my wife on the extension in the bedroom, telling her sister about the man she had been fucking for the last two months.

I quietly set the phone back down, and I went out my front door to sit on the steps. I stared into the lawn. It felt like I had been punched in the nose and had my heart ripped out. It hurt like Hell.

I had treated her like a queen. I was a good provider. We had good sex. Why?

The house went up for sale. The kids and I moved into an apartment. Every other weekend, the kids went to her apartment.

Sometimes on the weekends that I had the kids, I'd get a baby sitter and go out to the nightclubs with a buddy from work.

One night, I saw her there. She was with the guy she'd been fucking. They were all over each other. It was disgusting.

He was a classic Bad Boy—more precisely, a machismo asshole. He had all the smooth moves.

On one weekend when my wife had the kids, I went to the nightclubs, and I saw that guy. He was with another woman. He was doing to that woman what he had done to my wife.

He was startled when he turned to find me standing right in front of him. I assured him that I was not there to kill him, but simply to ask him something. I asked him what he had done right and I had done wrong.

Perhaps out of fear for his life, or maybe to brag, he told me everything.

He spoke in terms of examples. For educational purposes, I have distilled the morals of the examples here:

1) Find out what she needs and give it to her.

2) Women need constant reassurance, but, at the same time, constant doubt.

3) Never let her think she "has" you.

4) She must always be jealous of you.

5) Always remain interesting and challenging to her.

6) Always keep strife in the relationship.

7) Be possessive of her. She must feel "owned."

8) Never let her look at another man.

9) Keep other men away from her.

10) Show her more excitement than any other man has.

11) Sexually fulfill her, and then some.

12) Never let her feel she fully satisfies you.

13) Know her weaknesses and play them when needed.

Then he said, "I'm glad you're not the jealous type." I responded with, "If I were, you would not be here." He ran, because where he comes from, such matters are dealt with in very violent ways.

Here is an e-mail from a reader who misunderstood:

I am sure I am not alone when I ask; in your book you mentioned quote "Women need constant doubt" and "Never let her think she has you" unquote. Do I look at other women to make her think she is not the only one I desire? We have been married for 21 years and it seems I do not satisfy her any more as sex has dropped off to once a month or 2. Since reading your book I have managed to bring her to life in the 2 short times we have had sex (love). I have had a sheltered

```
life  and  need  help  to  hold  my  marriage
together. I need more. Please help.
```

Hopefully, that reader is alone in asking that question. I do not tell you to do those things. I merely tell you what that bad boy gave as advice. I also tell you in this book that you should NOT do those things and why.

Now, back to the story...

The following week, I had to drop off some papers at my wife's apartment. As I was about to knock on her door, I heard her and the Bad Boy inside having sex. She sounded like she was enjoying it a lot more than she had enjoyed sex with me. I listened until I heard her come very vocally, and then I slid the papers under the door and left.

Never again would a Bad Boy steal a woman away from me, and never again would a woman be anything less than completely fulfilled and breathless after sex with me.

CHAPTER 3
THE LONG ROAD TO ENLIGHTENMENT

"One night, I watched her at the window in her sleep. I noticed for the first time, how a woman's underclothes barely touches her skin. How it rides on a cushion of air as she moves. How the silk floats about her body, brushing her flesh like an angel's wings, and I understood how a woman must be touched."
~Don Juan DeMarco

I got my wits back and settled down. No longer was I interested in revenge. I simply wanted to be better and live a fulfilling life.

I knew what that Bad Boy was doing when he worked the women. I wanted to have the same effect on women, but I didn't want to do it by taking advantage of a woman's vulnerabilities. I wanted to do it by empowering her strengths.

I started by reading divorce recovery books. I read as many as I could.

That got me interested in books about relationships. I read tons of them.

It started to become apparent to me that my relationship with my wife had been doomed from the beginning. Basically, as it turned out, she had low self-esteem.

Even though she had the perfect life and was treated like a queen, she did not have the sense of deservedness enough to appreciate it. In fact, it was against what she believed that she deserved. She honestly believed that she deserved to be treated poorly. And thus, she sabotaged what she had with me.

So, basically, it was all my fault! I had chosen poorly!

That's right. I had only married her because she was so smoking hot.

That was the first step to recovery. I assumed responsibility for my lot in life.

Because of what I had been through, I worked hard to devise a way to choose the correct women, which has since served me well.

At the same time, I realized what that Bad Boy was doing. He was preying on the insecurities of women with low self-esteem.

"Women need constant doubt." "Never let her think she has you." That will certainly keep a woman with low self-esteem on her toes. Low self-esteem women are always chasing what they can't have. But a woman with high self-esteem will tire of that. A high self-esteem woman wants to get to the point where she can enjoy having her man. If she can't, she'll move on.

"She must always be jealous of you." This is true when preying on the insecurities of low self-esteem women, but very bad for women with high self-esteem. Life provides enough occasions for the "healthy" jealousy that keeps a relationship healthy.

"Always remain interesting and challenging to her." Agreed. However, there are healthy ways to do this.

"Always keep strife in the relationship." Wrong! That will attract low self-esteem "drama queens." It will repel high-quality women.

"Be possessive of her. She must feel owned." Very bad! High quality women do NOT want to be "owned." Later, I will explain the correct "occasional" context in which this is actually a good and very powerful thing.

"Never let her look at another man." "Keep other men away from her." Bad Boys are very insecure, paranoid men who know that other Bad Boys are always trying to steal their woman. In actuality, such a mind-set will repel high-quality women. In reality, there is no need!

"Show her more excitement than any other man has." "Sexually fulfill her, and then some." Agreed—most definitely. I have even gone MUCH further!

"Never let her feel she fully satisfies you." WRONG! In fact, when it comes to high-quality women, I will show you that you do indeed want to show her just how MUCH she satisfies you and why that is so powerful!

"Know her weaknesses and play them when needed." That is just so fucking stupid and typical of the low self-esteem Bad Boy.

I have devised much more rewarding ways to keep a woman with high self-esteem excited about the relationship, and in fact, to bring out her inner SLUT!

Since I was back in the dating scene again, I wanted to be a memorable lover for the women that I was meeting, and I also wanted to personally enjoy the experiences to the maximum extent possible. So, I read all the books about sexuality and being a better lover.

Unfortunately, they were somewhat disappointing.

On the weekends that the kids were at their mother's, I would go to the nightclubs.

At the time, I was 36 and felt old and used up. Then, I began to discover that some of the young women found me attractive. I started dating a 19-year-old woman who had gotten into the nightclub using a fake ID.

Unfortunately, she was not having orgasms. I was making love to her like I had made love to my wife for many years. I soon realized that that was not working on the new women.

Later, she started dating a Bad Boy. One night, she and I ran into each other, and I asked her how things were going. She was happy to report that her new boyfriend had given her her first orgasm!

Damnit! A Bad Boy had beaten me again!

I decided that that would never happen again.

I read more books on sexuality and being a better lover. I purchased educational videos. I listened to audio recordings. There may have been one paragraph in each book worth quoting, but, otherwise, they all rehashed the same old stuff.

I decided to try stuff myself and figure out what really works.

I started dating a 22-year-old woman. She also had never had an orgasm. She had only been with one man before. They had been together for a year, and no doubt he had tried everything on her.

So, I took my time finding what made her feel good. With my middle finger, I searched for her "G-spot," like all the sexuality books recommended, but I received no response from her.

Then, I decided to slide my finger in as far along the front wall of her vagina as I could. I curled the tip of my finger and pressed hard against the front wall. She immediately responded to this.

After continuing this for a few minutes, I watched the face of this beautiful woman while she experienced her very first orgasm.

It was beautiful to watch. It was wonderful to be there, to be a part of it, and to have helped to "facilitate."

I decided that I was going to be my own sexuality teacher.

I gave more women their first orgasm.

I converted women who had never masturbated in their life into masturbating maniacs.

I turned women who insisted that they could only have one orgasm into multi-orgasmic, come machines.

Interestingly, I later realized that I had actually benefited most from the education I received when I was writing my master's thesis in Electrical Engineering on Artificial Neural Networks.

As computer engineers, we looked to the human brain as an alternative computing architecture. It did things seemingly effortlessly that we could not get computers to do.

We read papers by neurologists. They quoted papers by psychiatrists and psychologists. That got me very interested in psychology.

I also learned some neural physiology and was starting to form an understanding of how the brain processes sexuality.

So, I started to look at the power in the psychology and neural physiology of female sexuality. That's when things got very interesting...

CHAPTER 4

WHAT I LEARNED FROM GIVING WOMEN PHONE SEX

"A woman will tell you everything you need to seduce her."
~Mark Cunningham

After my divorce in 1992, I felt very defeated and alone. I had custody of our two small children, and thus, I was stuck at home in the evenings. Hence, after I put the children to bed, I turned to the telephone.

There was a singles magazine in our area where people placed in personal ads. You read through the ads and decided which women to call. You then called a 900 number and left a message and your number. The ladies would then listen to their messages and decide who to call back.

That was back in the days before there was caller ID. The women could call and know that you had no way of knowing who they really were or where they lived, so there was that anonymity which gave them safety.

I picked women who were recently divorced and about 30 years old. When they would call, the rapport would build quickly because we had a lot in common and much to talk about.

I would build common ground based on our similar situations of having gone through a divorce. This allowed her to feel comfortable with me.

I also became very good at establishing an emotional connection with a woman on the telephone. This is critically important. Women are emotional creatures, and they need to establish a connection before they can feel free to continue further.

Since she understood my situation, I would say, "I really enjoy talking to you. I feel like I can tell you anything, and you understand it and accept it." She would reply, "Oh yes, I do!"

This served to make her feel that she could tell me anything, as well, and that I would fully understand it and accept it. Thus, she would open up even further.

By the end of their marriage, many of these women no longer felt sexual. They weren't having orgasms, even by masturbating. They didn't even fantasize. There was no point in it.

They had left their marriages for various reasons, but in all cases, the sex had become boring. Their husbands were lousy lovers. I asked these women, "Was it because he had a small penis?" They replied, "Well, actually, no."

Many of them had affairs with exciting lovers. They talked about how much their lover turned them on. I asked them, "Was it because he had a big penis?" They replied, "Well, actually, no."

Apparently, it didn't have anything to do with the size of the man's penis.

All of my preexisting beliefs about sexuality began to crumble.

So far, this may sound as if I was being very pathetic, and as I look back on it, I can see it that way.

However, hearing these women's stories was fascinating to me.

It was also therapeutic for me. It was sort of a "mutually helpful divorce recovery program." It helped me to deal with my recent divorce. Also, I have to admit, it helped with the loneliness.

The women were lonely, too. They were reaching out in the dark to talk to another human being, to have thoughtful human interaction.

For them, it was also therapeutic to share their secrets, even with an anonymous person; and because it was anonymous, they were completely open and honest.

I was learning a lot. The stories were very revealing, and quite fascinating.

I became very good at getting them to open up and share.

I would ask them, "What do you really want in a man?" They would describe, or at least try to describe, what they wanted to the best of their ability. Often, they didn't really know themselves; they just knew what they wanted to feel. The important thing is that they started to feel those feelings while they were on the phone with me.

So, I would then ask, "How would it make you feel to be with such a man?" They would describe that. In order to do so, they had to imagine feeling it. This caused them to actually begin to feel those feelings and imagine that they were really with that man. Because they were talking to me and had rapport with me, those feelings got associated to me on a subconscious level. They did not realize this on a conscious level.

Because I was genuinely interested in what they thought and because I made it a point to demonstrate that I was a good listener, they opened up about what they would really like to have—in other words, what they fantasized about on an emotional and relationship basis.

When they were basking in a flood of good emotions and feelings, which were all connected to me, I would ramp that up. After having established an emotional connection with them that allowed them to feel very close to me, I leveraged that to move the conversation in a romantic direction.

I would ask them to describe what they would do on the ideal "date." They would describe some romantic night out, consisting of dinner, dancing, and walking on the beach. Of course, they gave me detailed descriptions. "Then, we are seated at our table, which is adorned with a fine white linen tablecloth and one tall candle."

Sometimes, they would instead prefer that I describe the ideal date. If so, I would simply narrate the ideal date as described to me by previous women. It's simple really—give women what they have to have.

After they were basking in the flood of romantic feelings, all of which were linked to me, allowing them to feel romantic toward me, I covertly moved things in a sexual direction.

I would ask, "Do you ever feel alone?" They would affirm.

Then, I posed these questions: "What would it feel like to be the opposite of alone? What word could be used to describe that?"

They would try to describe it and put a word to it. It served to remind them that they were alone and how much they yearned to feel close and connected.

Then, I would say, "Yeah. Sometimes I feel alone, especially at this time of night. I think about what it would be like to be with that someone special. What would we say? What would we do? How would we make each other feel?"

They would softly agree, "Yeah..."

Then, I'd continue, "I feel very close to you right now." They would reply, "Yes, I feel very close to you, too."

Then, I would softly say, "I wish I were there with you right now." They would softly reply, "Yes..."

"If I were there right now, I would want to hold you so close." They softly replied, "Yeah..."

"And I would feel your soft skin against mine." They would sigh.

Here is the critical point...

"And I would ever-so-softly kiss the side of your neck."

At this point, 80 percent of the women would simply stop talking and just sigh.

I would continue...

"And I would softly kiss the side of your neck all the way down to your shoulder."

I would slowly describe in detail everything I would do if I were there, beginning with what I would kiss, then what I would touch.

They would moan.

Then, I told them what I would lick.

Within minutes, these women would be screaming in orgasmic ecstasy.

These women were all attractive and educated. On the very first call, fully 80% of them would engage in phone sex with me, a man they have never talked to before in their life.

Have you ever heard of anything like that before? Intelligent, educated, professional, successful, attractive women calling a strange man and having phone sex? It's usually the other way around, where men pay $4.99 a minute to call a woman to have phone sex.

I continually adjusted and refined my phone sex techniques, making them progressively more realistic and effective. Just from my voice and the reality that I created in their mind with sensory rich descriptions, erotic words, and eventually outright naughty vulgarity, women were having orgasms. Then women were having multiple orgasms; then women were having orgasms without even touching themselves.

I became extremely good at giving phone sex. I was absolutely lethal. The phone would ring, and I knew that within one hour another woman who I had never talked to before would be screaming in orgasmic ecstasy.

It became routine. I had to work the next day, and I needed a freshly ironed shirt for work, so I'd be getting women off on the phone while I was ironing my shirts. I would literally be having phone sex while I did my laundry!

Picture this... I am looking down at my ironing board, holding the collar of my white shirt down with my left hand, while my right hand pressed the iron across my shirt. The phone was pinched between my right shoulder and chin, while I said, "Keep coming for me, Baby! I'm gonna come! Now! NOW, Baby! Come harder!" Meanwhile, the woman was screaming at the top of her lungs right into my ear.

I was leading a private life, running a phone sex line for women in the evenings. But I knew I was onto something.

These women were well-educated professionals—elementary school teachers, mid-level managers, emergency room nurses, stockbrokers, sales directors, fast-rising corporate executives, you name it. They all had high self-esteem. They came from good homes. They were the farthest thing from sluts. When I got on the phone with them, however, and unlocked their pent-up sexual potential, they became very slutty.

These women really opened up and taught me things that fascinated me. They spoke of their sexual past and their fantasies. I learned a great deal about the secret sexual lives and thoughts of women from all of those conversations. That's when I really started to understand the underlying sexual potential that exists within women.

My beliefs about women were shattered and totally rewritten. I became even more fascinated with the minds of women.

Women are not that complicated, after all. It's just that we don't understand them. That is completely understandable, considering the fact that social conditioning has misled us. Even some of the so-called "sex experts" had unintentionally misguided us through their own ignorance or political correctness.

I am trying to get you to begin to understand women and to rewrite your own beliefs. When you truly begin to understand women, they are no longer intimidating, but instead, they are absolutely fascinating and thoroughly enjoyable.

The interesting thing is that even during my "phone sex period," I began to understand that what I was doing was something very novel. I was onto something that nobody knew about. There was nobody who I could talk to about it because nobody could even comprehend that it was even possible.

And, I had absolutely no idea at the time that I would end up teaching this stuff. I just wanted to learn.

At the time, I was on the beginning of a long learning curve that would prove to be the beginning of a fascinating journey.

CHAPTER 5

TEN THINGS WOMEN LOVE. . . BUT WOULD NEVER ADMIT

"To love is to live on the precipice."
~Pauline Reage

It seemed like everything that society told us was a lie.

Movies, television shows, stories, other people, our parents, women, and all that "social conditioning" told us that we had to talk women into having sex. It almost made it seem as if sex for a woman was a chore she performed, an obligation she fulfilled, only as a reward for us spending money and attention on her.

That single misguided piece of social conditioning had me perplexed for years.

It was a belief that was hindering me, a self-defeating belief. I was determined to crush it by finding the truth, and then to replace that belief with empowering beliefs based on reality.

I realized that all the social conditioning was not jiving with what was actually happening in reality.

During my 20s, most of my girlfriends absolutely loved sex. It's not that they initiated it, but they would hint at it, and then the moment I would initiate it, they would jump on it. Then, in my marriage, my wife had to have it every single night. From my point of view, it appeared that women loved sex.

So, in my phone sex phase after my divorce, I tried a cruel experiment. I met with some of the women I talked with on the phone. We'd meet at a neutral place, have a drink, and then go to her place.

I would get her naked on the bed, and then I'd hesitate. I'd stall for as long as I could. If she persisted further, I'd say, "I'm not really ready for this yet," or, "I think maybe this is moving too quickly." Basically, I was purposely NOT going to have sex with her, just to see what would happen.

What happened was that they got PISSED! Either they'd be insulted and start sulking or they'd cuss me out. One woman even called me a coward! I made peace with them, got back on their good side, and then obliged them. Then, they went at it to such a degree as to make themselves look selfish.

I laugh now as I look back on it, but it proved something very important to me:

Women Love Sex!

Women actually WANT to have sex! Not merely as a reward to 'a nice guy,' but simply because WOMEN LOVE SEX!

(That does NOT mean that women are promiscuous.)

That, along with the stories that women shared with me over the phone and with all the factual evidence from reality, clearly showed that not only do women love sex, but, in fact, women are far more 'sexual' than men.

Further evidence of this can be found in any woman's fantasy book, such as "*My Secret Garden*" by Nancy Friday. That will open your eyes. Women have elaborate, intricate fantasies beyond anything men can imagine. For women, it is largely mental and emotional and about being "taken" and "ravished."

So, more accurately...

Women Love To Get FUCKED!

That does NOT mean that women want to be raped—certainly NOT!

On the other hand, in the context of consent, mental stimulation, emotional rapport, and trust, women love to be taken and ravished and fucked hard by their men.

I always thought that women only liked to "make sweet love." They certainly sometimes do, as do I, but they sometimes also like to get fucked! So, I started doing that, and they got crazy!

I pushed the envelope even further. While fucking them hard, I would talk dirty. They got crazier!

During my last two years of college, I had a college sweetheart who I found to be very cute and sexy. She also happened to be very intelligent, had very high self-esteem, and was extremely sexual.

We had very good sex. We did it often and always had simultaneous orgasms.

One day, she said to me, "As you know, I love horses. Well, I also admire how they are very animalistic when they have sex. When we do it doggy style, I sometimes imagine that I am a horse and that I am being very animalistic."

I couldn't believe what I was hearing, but, of course, I said, "Oh good, Baby, I love that you are able to feel animalistic."

I had certainly heard that women like to be "animalistic." I never really thought that they went as far as to imagine they were an animal!

So, the next time we did it doggy style, I said to her, "Oh yeah, Baby, you are being very animalistic!"

She got even more excited. I couldn't believe I was saying this.

I took a big gulp of courage and said, "You are so animalistic, just like a horse. Whinny like a horse!"

She started making horse noises! She started going crazy!

What do horses do? Whinny? I don't know.

I continued, "Oh yeah, Baby, make like a horse! You're getting fucked like an animal!"

She went ballistic. She started screaming in orgasmic ecstasy.

I couldn't believe it. It was so "foreign" to me, but hell, it worked, and very powerfully. Truth is found in reality.

My next girlfriend had no interest in horses, but she did like to be animalistic. I altered what I said to fit the situation. It worked amazingly well.

I was onto something. I varied it further with each subsequent girlfriend. I moved it from being animalistic to being slutty. That worked even better.

I found that the more vulgar and raunchy I got, the more excited they would get.

Women Love Dirty Talk!

I pushed the envelope even further. I would see how very naughty I could make them be.

I would make a fantasy scenario where she is a very naughty little schoolgirl who was caught masturbating, and I am the mean, disciplinary principal. I would spank her and tell her how naughty she is and that she needs to be disciplined. "You're being very naughty! You will learn to be a good girl! You are being so naughty, but you want to be a good girl! Come like a good girl!" This would consistently result in powerful orgasms.

One woman I dated was the executive assistant for the president of a huge corporation. She was very proper and conservative and wore Liz Claiborne suits. She owned a condo on a lake. I would take her out to the beach and fuck her on the picnic table where anyone with binoculars could see. I told her, "You love getting fucked where everyone can see you. You are so very naughty!"

Then, I brought her into her condo and fucked her in every room of her house, while telling her, "You love to get fucked! You can't get fucked enough!" She would almost lose consciousness with the long string of orgasms.

Women Love to be Naughty!

I wanted to see how naughty I could make them be, even to the point of doing very taboo things.

Anal sex has always been a man's fantasy, but I thought women didn't want to have anything to do with it. How wrong I was.

I would make them feel very naughty, and then I'd use that to tell them that they are even naughtier because they want to be very taboo and get fucked up the ass.

Then, I'd train them to have anal orgasms, and they would insist on being fucked up the ass! Very taboo.

Women Love to be Taboo!

I had read stories about women being tied up, so I tried that.

I would tie her hands to the bedposts so that her arms were outstretched and she was restrained to the bed, unable to get away. Then, I'd remind her how she is so very helpless and that I intended to do with her as I pleased and have my way with her.

Then, I'd tease her with oral stimulation and hold her right on the edge. Then, I'd ravish her by fucking her hard, which always resulted in spectacular orgasms. They loved it!

Women Love to be Dominated!

I pushed things further, even to the point of making her seem like a slut. I found that women responded powerfully to that.

While fucking them doggy style up the ass and pulling their hair, I'd tell women, "You love to get fucked up the ass like the slut that you are!" They got even crazier!

As an extreme example of making a woman become a total slut, I brought one girlfriend to an on-premise swinger's club, where sexual intercourse among couples happens in a large room as others watch.

I had her select a single man who she found attractive, and then he and I double penetrated her while everybody watched and I said to her, "You love to get fucked hard by two men! Show me how you love to get fucked! You love getting fucked hard like the slut that you are!" She was screaming in continuous simultaneous vaginal and anal orgasms.

Needless to say, she became even more wildly crazy about me. Powerful stuff.

It just goes to show...

Women Love to Get Slutty!

Now, that does NOT mean that women want to BE sluts (in a derogatory way). Certainly NOT! However, in the correct context, with her trusted lover, women love to become ruthlessly expressive sexual creatures.

It appears that anything that is taboo is even more exciting, simply because it IS forbidden. It is that contrast, that dichotomy.

Simply the fact that it smacks at the general definition of what it means to be a "proper" woman is what makes it exciting.

Moreover, interestingly, the better the sex is, the more she has to have it!

You might think that when a woman is getting really good sex, she would be satisfied and not need it more often. That could not be further from the truth. In actuality, when a woman is wildly crazy about her man and the sex is fantastic, she gets even hornier. She can't get it enough!

Women are Horny Monsters!

In many cases, women are far hornier than men. One woman I knew who was in her late 30s told me, "I get so damn horny! I feel like a 16-year-old boy. It's not fair!" Another woman told me, "It gets worse at the time I ovulate. Every man I see with a cute butt I want to jump him right then and there and ride him hard!"

Even so, women ONLY do these things when led by a man. They cannot do it themselves. They cannot initiate themselves. They can't even suggest it because that would be contrary to being a woman. She needs a man to lead her.

Women NEED Men!

Where is she going to find such a man? Men like this are extremely rare. That's what makes the Masterful Lover such a precious find.

Now, let's get back to social conditioning.

Why did all that social conditioning want us to believe that women didn't like sex very much? It appears that there are a number of reasons for this.

Social conditioning protects women from men who only want to use women for sex. If social conditioning trains people to believe that women must first be in love to have sex or that they must first be in a committed relationship, then women always have a defense against men who view women as simply objects. Rightly so.

It keeps teenagers in check. Parents teach their children that sex is only for love and marriage so their children won't go out and have sex and end up with teenage pregnancies.

Interestingly, the social conditioning does parallel the reality of being a woman to some degree. What I mean by that is the following. Most women are sexually submissive. They do not initiate sex. Instead, they respond to their man when he initiates. Most women prefer it that way. Women are excited by the fact that they excite their man. Women love to be desired and "taken" by their man. It makes them feel feminine and beautiful.

Unfortunately, though, women are also victims of social conditioning. Social conditioning is interpreted to mean that any woman who loves sex must be a slut. This has caused great frustration for women.

Even though women love sex, they'd never admit it to a stranger. It would make them appear to be a slut. It would also invite advances from men who objectify women.

The advantage of all this social conditioning is that, since it is against social norms for a woman to love sex, it makes it even more exciting WHEN a woman demonstrates that she loves sex. Anything that is taboo is even MORE exciting because it IS taboo.

Women Love Taboos!

To further complicate things, most of us men have been raised to be proper, polite gentlemen, and we have been taught that to suggest sex to a woman would insult her because it would insinuate that she is a slut.

That piece of social conditioning hinders men and puts men in a predicament. A man wants to be sexual with the woman he is interested in, but he can't suggest it because it would insult her.

The woman certainly can't suggest it because that would define her as a slut. Besides, women are sexually submissive. They prefer that the man initiate.

But women want their man to suggest it, because women love sex.

Here is the most important thing that men need to understand, yet, it is one of the toughest things for men to accept...

Women are far more sexual than men

In fact, women are far more sexual than most men can even comprehend.

CHAPTER 6
WHAT WOMEN WANT

"A woman is a mystery to be solved. But a woman holds nothing from a true lover. Like the blush of a rose, pink and pale, she must be coaxed to open her petals with a warmth like the sun. It calls for the lust of a whale crashing to the shore, so we may steal up what lies beneath, and bring the foamy delight of passion to the surface."
~Don Juan DeMarco

What do women want? It is an age-old question.

Don't ask women. When women are asked what they look for in a man, they usually say something like "a sense of humor" or "a nice guy," but that is not really what they respond to. Women respond to feelings.

Every woman grew up knowing exactly how it would feel to have the ideal man. It is that feeling she must have when a handsome stranger sweeps her off her feet. A woman does not choose a man because of who he is; she chooses him because of how it makes her feel.

To find what it is that women want, we must look at what women actually respond to. Truth is found in reality, and reality is there for all of us to observe.

We begin looking for the answer by observing the various men that a woman has been with in her life.

THE BAD BOY

The bad boy gives her exciting sex, and because he is very masculine, he makes her feel sexy. However, he is a self-absorbed jerk who cheats on her. She does not feel appreciated, and she probably is unable to feel any emotional connection. She often becomes addicted to him because the sex is so good and she feels so very sexual. She will try in vain to tame him, but it is fruitless. In an emotional breakup, she finally leaves him for good—at least the high self-esteem woman finally leaves him for good.

You may be asking, "Are there lots of women that don't like the aggressive bad boy attitude at all? What about the important aspect of politeness and manners?"

A lot of women are turned off by the aggressive attitude of bad boys, if by "aggressive" you mean rude and pushy, and if the context is outside the bedroom in social situations.

Outside of the bedroom and in social interactions, most women prefer "politeness and manners." It's just human nature.

Still, as you look around, you find that bad boys tend to get the girls, while nice guys don't. Women are often seen crying on the shoulder of a nice guy "friend" as she suffers through the extreme emotional highs and lows of a relationship with a bad boy "lover."

Bad boys are aggressive. Nice guys are polite. Thus, a lot of "reforming nice guys" who want to be "exciting bad boys" will try to act aggressive, but they just end up being rude wimps.

A lot of it has to do with context. As I have previously discussed at length, women want to be treated like a lady in the living room and ravished like the slut that they love to be in the bedroom.

Women know that bad boys can ravish them, and I'm talking about the dangerous-to-know, impossible-to-tame bad boy. (Also, I'm talking about MOST women, at least once in their lives.)

Bad boys are exciting. For a woman, the sex is awesome with a bad boy. He is dominant, he talks dirty to her, he makes her do things she is too inhibited to do, and she loves it. It makes her feel sexual. It is extremely exciting for a woman to experience those intense sexual feelings.

Bad boys are masculine. The feminine in a woman is attracted to the masculine in a man, and with a bad boy, it is extreme. It is this contrast that is so alluring to a woman. It makes her feel sexy and feminine.

Bad boys lead an exciting life. They are daring and live on the edge. Women want to be part of it to make their own life more exciting.

Bad boys are mysterious. They have a dark side that women are endlessly curious to know. She never really feels she knows him.

Bad boys cannot be tamed. Women are nurturing creatures, and are thus compelled to save him. She is determined to rescue him by teaching him how to love.

Bad boys are fearless with women. He will woo her by being sweet and gentlemanly, while she is drawn to his masculine confidence.

Bad boys are addictive. She becomes so wrapped up in her experience that she realizes she needs it, and the bad boy knows it.

Once she becomes addicted, the bad side of the bad boy comes out.

Bad boys are selfish. He inconsiderately takes and takes, and she gladly gives and gives even more in order to keep him because she is addicted to the exciting sex.

Bad boys are secretive. She begins to notice things he is keeping from her, things about his dark side that would be self-incriminating.

Bad boys make promises of fidelity and then deny their indiscretions. When she learns he has cheated, she is hurt; but she needs it, so she works even harder to save him.

Bad boys are paranoid. He knows that other men do exactly the same thing. Thus, he becomes very jealous and possessive of his women. He becomes controlling in order to keep her to himself.

It is incongruent. The internal incongruity is another form of weakness.

Most every highly-sexual woman has been with a bad boy at least once in her life. This is true for both high self-esteem and low self-esteem women.

Eventually, the high self-esteem woman can't take the drama any more, and she leaves him. It is probably the most emotionally traumatic thing she will ever do. It is heart wrenching for her because she has become so addicted to the awesome sex.

After a woman has been through the roller coaster ride with a bad boy, she will forever avoid inconsiderate jerks, but she will always crave those intense sexual feelings.

Let me repeat: She will ALWAYS crave those intense sexual feelings.

Here is a comment from a woman in response to my Youtube video:

```
OMG your so right about us women craving the
"bad boy"! My ex was a "bad boy" and I stuck
with him for 5 years and put up with so much
crap from him, and I haven't been with him
or a "bad boy" for nearly 3 years now, but
that "bad boy" craving is still very strong,
probably will have it forever.
```

It is because she craves those intense sexual feelings that there is a tremendous opportunity for you. So, you can thank the bad boys for doing some of the preparation work for you.

I have studied the bad boys for many years because I wanted to have the same kind of powerful sexual affect on women, but I was determined to go beyond that. I was going to figure out everything it takes to have that powerful affect on a woman and still have all the other things that a woman must have, because when all those other things are true...

It makes the sex even more awesome.

So, when you step into a woman's life, she sees that she could have all the things she has always wanted, and she begins to become excited about the possibilities.

THE NICE GUY

Then there's the classic nice guy wimp. He makes her feel appreciated, and he is able to establish an emotional connection with her. Unfortunately, though, he's boring or he's not masculine, so she doesn't feel sexy and doesn't feel turned on about sex. She'd love to marry him, because he'd be perfect for a family, but for some reason, she keeps delaying the engagement. It's because he doesn't make her feel like a sexual creature.

Here is a letter from a woman ranting about her "nice guy" boyfriend. She posted it on craigslist.org, September 10, 2006.

Why nice guys SUCK

This is a long rant, so bear with me or hit your back button. I'm frustrated and in no mood for your shit either, so if you don't want to read it, well...

So I'm dating a nice guy now and it SUCKS. No other way to explain it, it just SUCKS. He's no challenge. He agrees with everything I say. He's got it all though - a decent job, a nice house, no kids, no psycho ex-wives, and he's tall and cute. Anyone ever seen that Friends episode when Alec Baldwin played Phoebe's boyfriend?

YEAH, my boyfriend is THAT nice. He's just too fucking nice. Nice is boring. I've never heard him raise his voice. He's never aggressive. He has no edge. He won't even drive over the speed limit and that fucking annoys the shit out of me, yet I sit in the passenger seat and keep my mouth shut... watching everyone whiz by us.

Don't get me started on the sex. Oh, excuse me... making love. After he cums (note I didn't mention anything about ME cumming), he rolls over and says, "Oh, that was nice," with a little sigh. I KID YOU NOT, he says it EVERY TIME and then he sighs like he has just woken from a refreshing nap. I finally got so tired of missionary and him looking lovingly into my eyes and smiling as he came, that I threw him down on the couch one night and mounted him. At first he was terrified - yes, TERRIFIED. He thought something had possessed me.

It HAD -- it was sheer MADNESS. I fucked the shit out of him that night. He then sighed and said, "Oh, that was nice."

Now that we had the cowgirl position conquered (always with that sigh afterwards), it was time to move on to doggie. His ex-girlfriend never did doggie. (Hmmm... maybe there's a "nice" ex-girlfriend to blame for his timid niceness? That bitch...) Anyway, I digress. I tell him I want him to fuck me from behind. Yes, I used the word "fuck" and I didn't care what he thought about it. He gets behind me and enters me, and damned if he didn't say, "OH, THIS IS NICE"!!! Are there any 35 y/o men out there that haven't smacked a woman's ass when doing her doggie? YES, and he's my boyfriend!

Tonight during sex, I think I'm gonna tell him to stick his finger in my ass when I'm riding him. THAT should be interesting.

So for the nice guys out there, my advice is this: It's great that you're nice (to an extent), but have some backbone. Don't be a spine donor all your life. When your girl is out of line, say something. Don't let her walk all over you. Occasionally, be a "bad" boy (being bad doesn't translate to abusive or criminal). Say "No" to her sometimes. Raise your voice and be heard. Say something dirty/sexy to her occasionally. Drink a few too many beers and piss out in public. Smack her ass.

Don't ever use the word NICE to describe things, especially sex (okay, that may be a personal pet peeve).

Have an interest in at LEAST one sport (or pretend to).

Drive 5-10 miles over the speed limit once in awhile.

Run an old lady off the road just for kicks (yeah, I'm kidding about this one... just ride her bumper for a few miles).

Be aggressive during sex. Take off those damn white socks and Jesus sandals.

Grow a goatee for a few weeks. Shave your balls. Stray from your routine and shake things up.

BE A MAN FOR GOD'S SAKE... and the women will fall at your feet.

Whew... THAT FELT NICE.

All too typical. That woman is in the process of dumping her man, and she may not even realize it yet.

It happens often. The woman becomes frustrated that the man does not see the sexual creature in her. She still cares about him, but she no longer responds sexually to him. Thus, she loses respect for him.

Out of her frustration, she then goes into a stage where she mocks his ignorance and shocks him by making HIM do taboo things. After she has entertained herself for some time, she finds that she has lost all respect for him, and she dumps him.

THE EMOTIONALLY UNAVAILABLE GUY

The closest she might get to the ideal relationship is the emotionally unavailable guy. He's not a wimp, and he's not a jerk. He may be masculine and give her good sex. He may be a gentleman and make her feel very appreciated. Still, there's one important thing missing; he's not emotionally available. She never feels emotionally connected to him. This is probably the biggest complaint women have. She found the ideal guy in all respects, but damnit, he's not emotionally available. She tries over and over to get him to open up to her, but it never happens. Women are emotional creatures, and they need it, so she eventually leaves.

THE GAY FRIEND

There are other men in her life. There's her gay friend. She loves hanging out with him because he makes her feel special and appreciated. They have an emotional bond, and they talk about everything. She feels very close to him, but damnit, he's gay, and, thus, not an option.

THE MYSTERIOUS LOVER

Then, there's the occasional mysterious lover. For many reasons, she'd never ever consider him seriously for anything, but damn, the sex is good. Once every few months, when she is bored with how things are going for her, she'll call him up and go over for one thing and one thing only: sex. Then she leaves, hoping she will soon find the ideal man.

THE MARRIED MAN

Finally, as one last example, there's the married man. Only low self-esteem women allow themselves to become a mistress, or in other words, a woman who wants what she can't have. He gives her exciting sex, makes her feel sexy, and they share a deep emotional connection; but he won't leave his wife, so she doesn't feel special. Because she has low self-esteem, it is very difficult for her to leave.

Let's get back to high self-esteem women.

Those were examples of men in her life. As you can see, one or more of her needs are not being met in each example. By looking at what is missing, we learn more about what she has to have.

When you observe relationships, you find that some relationships are more fulfilling and successful than others. In the successful relationships, both people are getting all the things they need. In the relationships that are not fulfilling, the needs of one or both of the people are not being met. This gives us a clue as to what women need.

When you observe women who went outside of their marriage, you find that they are obtaining that which they were missing in their marriage. For example, if the sex is boring, she will get an exciting lover. If the sex in the marriage is acceptable, but she feels that she is not being treated with respect, she will find a man who will treat her with respect. If she does not have emotional intimacy in her marriage, she will have an emotional affair. When women go outside of their marriage, they are looking to have one or more of their needs met. For some women, if it takes two different men in order to get all her needs met, she'll do it.

So, to learn more about what women want, we look at why women cheat.

Susan Shapiro Barash wrote a fascinating book called "*A Passion for More*," which sheds light on the dark side of female sexuality. It includes the interviews of 57 women who had extramarital affairs.

Every woman interviewed had something missing in her marriage. Each woman filled the missing need by taking a lover. Some of the women felt guilt about it, but most did not. In all cases, the women were happy they did it, as it ultimately led her to greater enlightenment and fulfillment.

Almost all of the women had much better sex with their lover than with their husband. For a few of the women, the sex was better with the husband, and the affair ended. In all cases, the woman's thoughts were consumed with the man that she had the most exciting sex with.

Some women had great sex with a man because she felt close to him. For most of the women, she became close to him because she had great sex with him.

I have taken a few quotes from "*A Passion for More*" to give you a flavor for the book. Because these are very minimal quotes, they are thus by definition taken out of context. Certainly, each woman's situation was more involved, but it gives you an idea...

Honey: "*The affair awakened me sexually. I felt more uninhibited with my lover than with my husband. We had anal sex. He was a superb lover. I could have multiple orgasms with him, which wasn't happening in my marriage at the time. I was obsessed with him when he wasn't around, although we were together a few days a week.*"

Lucy: "*The sex was excellent because he was so skilled. It was a learning experience for me. At first I slept with both my husband and this man; eventually I had sex only with my lover. It was hot. We had sex every possible way. For almost a year there was an intense, hot situation. The sex was wild and continual.*"

Sandy: "*It was a wonderful sexual and emotional union and I never felt guilty. My lover adored me. He thought I was beautiful and gave me everything I wanted. The sex was loving and gentle but also uninhibited and open. We'd have sex everywhere. We did it in restaurants, in the back of the movie theatre. Wherever we were, we did it. If we went away, we'd do it on a mountain cliff, in the beach, in the car all the time, in the buggy ride in the city.*"

Hanna: "*The sex was very exciting in the beginning. I'd see him daily sometimes, other times a few days a week, so there was lots of sex. Because he accepted me, I was able to play out sexual fantasies. The fantasies were things I would have done with my husband if he'd been willing, but with my lover there was no question that he was willing. My relationship with my lover made me see myself as a whole*" *person and I rejected my husband's needs. My lover was reinforcing. He made me feel beautiful."*

Rebecca: *"Sex with my lover was very different than with my husband. Now I think of my lover as very handsome, but in the beginning my husband seemed handsomer."*

In every one of the 57 cases, the married woman was not getting one or more of the things that a woman must have. With her lover, she could get the thing or things that she was not getting with her husband. For some women, if it takes two different men in order to get all her needs met, she'll do it.

In every single case where the woman went outside her marriage, she did it to meet one or more of the following needs:

1) To feel special

2) To feel a deep emotional connection

3) To feel like a woman

4) To have passionate sex

As a result, we can conclude what women must have four things...

THE FOUR THINGS WOMEN MUST HAVE

First, a woman needs to feel appreciated for the unique individual that she is. She needs to feel special, unlike any other woman, and she needs to know that her man supports her in her endeavors.

Second, she needs to feel that deep, intimate emotional connection. She needs to have that emotional intimacy with her man. It's a connection she shares only with him.

Third, she needs to feel like a woman. She needs to feel beautiful, sexy, and feminine. She needs to enjoy all those things that come with being a woman.

Finally, she needs hot, passionate sex. She needs to be seduced, enticed, teased, and satisfied, over and over again. She needs to experience new things, in new ways, including fantasies and roles. It makes her feel desired, affirmed, and alive.

This is verified by reflecting back on the men in a woman's life. We find that each of them met some, but not all, of the four needs. The nice guy made her feel special and had an emotional connection with her. The bad boy made her feel sexy and gave her passionate sex. Neither of them gave her the four things she needs.

In every case where the woman went outside her marriage, the woman was consumed with thoughts of the man who was the exciting lover. I get e-mails from such women regularly. Here is one such e-mail:

> My boss where I used to work, his name was David Shade, and all the guys used to snicker about his name and no one would tell me why, because I was the only woman attorney. One day I asked one of the senior partner attorneys, and he told me to check his name on the internet, and then I found your web site. Very interesting.
>
> I have been married for 20 years. I have been bored for the last 10 years, and I am ready to ask for a divorce. I met a man, and after less than 2 months with him I am crazy in love with him.
>
> The sex is great. We are crazy in love with each other. We talk about everything and share everything we think and feel without hesitation. He is very sensitive and very much a man at the same time.
>
> Both of us are very sexual and have connected to the things in the bedroom that turns us on, and we share them with each other. We have questioned the sex part over and over because it is the best we have ever had with anyone. All we know is that we turn each other on in ways we have never experienced.

Both of our marriages (both of us are married) are pretty much over and were really over before we met. Our marriages were over because of communication and sex not happening. So we have come to the conclusion that sex and communication now is the reason why we are so crazy in love, because we don't have it and have not had it for years with our spouses.

Well, this guy is the first one I have had and the first time I have cheated on my husband, and for some reason I do not feel guilty about it.

I bought your books and I am giving them to my lover.

He actually already understands 80% of this because he makes me feel like a woman that I have never felt in me before. I do not really think he needs these books, but this is really a gift to him to let him know he already has most all of it. This will give him even more confidence as a man in loving me and knowing that the woman in me really wants and needs all that is written in your books. I have felt it inside of me for a long time and this guy brings it all out. What a beautiful feeling it is.

I am learning about myself as well through them. Yes I am a naughty girl too :) but a professional during the day :)

Reading your material is giving me a window of understanding to know what I need to do differently for me to ultimately enjoy and have a very connected relationship with my new lover.

Good looks and love are not enough if the sex is lame. Here is an e-mail from Lisa:

David,

You are so right about the four things that a woman must have.

My last relationship was very loving and romantic. He was very good to me, and I loved him.

We could talk literally for hours. We would spontaneously dance in the living room. We were always touching each other. We would give each other "the look" and know exactly what we were communicating to each other.

The sex was always very loving and romantic... but the sex was ALWAYS very loving and romantic. There was never any variation whatsoever. We never talked in bed. It was always quiet and dark. It was never in the day.

Hence, I cheated on him all the time. One man, who was very exciting, gave me my first orgasm in intercourse. Then I'd go back to my boyfriend for all the other stuff. I never had orgasms in intercourse with him.

I am physically attracted to him. He works out five times a week. He just doesn't do it for me sexually.

Guilt got me. He is a good man and doesn't deserve to be treated like this, so I let him go. It was the hardest thing I ever did.

What is left is two people who love each other, who have a bond, but can't be together.

He now has a woman living with him. I get jealous that he is with her sexually. I know he just has her to have somebody, but I know she isn't good enough for him, and she is jealous of me, because she knows that he is still in love with me.

I miss him, but I know it would never work with him.

Here is an e-mail from Janice:

Hello David,

I'm semi-happily married to my husband with whom I share many interests but he lacks any style in the bedroom. He has not been able to bring me to orgasm ever in eleven years of being together.

I have bought toys to help and he actually gets jealous of them. I did tell him I like dirty talk and all the other things I know I like.

I even bought your CD's Dirty Talk and he hasn't picked them up to listen to them yet. He actually acted hurt over my suggestions of listening to them.

I have been chatting with another male friend who sounds like he knows very well how to please a woman and tells me all the things he would do to me. I have been very tempted to be with him but know it's not really going to help my situation at home.

Then sometimes I think having a lover to satisfy my needs on the side is just what I need. This other person is only looking to sexually gratify me, nothing else.

I'm wondering if there is something else I can do to convince my husband to take my subtle clues I need him to be more interested in satisfying me. He does oral for maybe three minutes then wham bam thank you mam.

I'm VERY frustrated all the time!! Help me because I'm soooo tempted to take this other man up on his offer.

Here is an e-mail from Cathy:

Hi David,

I'm a 38 year old woman with two kids. I have been very dissatisfied with the sexual side of my marriage. In 15 years, my husband has never given me an orgasm.

Mind you, I can have both clitoral and vaginal orgasms on my own. So I know that there is nothing physically wrong with me. And even though everything else about him is great, I've been contemplating leaving because I do not want to live the rest of my life without having someone to explore my sexuality with.

So...I have been trying to open my husband's mind up to new things...talking dirty, using toys, role playing and pleasure outside of straight intercourse. Over the years, I have at times tried to slowly engage my husband in one or the other of these ideas and he seems very turned off and defensive. Then I feel bad and back off a bit.

Of course, by now, I am very frustrated and at the end of my rope. I have promised myself to give the marriage one more shot and this is it. So...how can I get him to understand how vital it is to me that I can be with a man who is willing to understand and explore my sexuality with me without facing the barrier of his ego?

And at this point, I won't just be satisfied with orgasms. I want the whole package; dirty talk, kinky sex, role playing, etc. It's all or nothing and the marriage depends on it.

Thank you.

And here is a letter from a man who has benefited from the ignorance and neglect of married men. This letter appeared in Playboy Advisor:

I'm a single, average-looking businessman in my mid-forties.

During the past three years I've slept with every married woman I have desired.

I meet them in super markets, bookstores, and record shops.

I invite them for coffee, and the rest is easy.

From these encounters, I have observed the following:

1. I've not met a woman whose husband has made love to her properly in the past six months.

2. Many of these women had never had a multiple orgasm. Two had never had orgasms until we went to bed.

3. None of these women experienced any major guilt from these encounters.

4. Most view they are neglected and view our time as luxurious sin.

In the meantime, I've collected a casual harem.

I'm never pushy; they call me.

Can you explain why so many men are such neglectful lovers?

Signed T.G.

That letter was not to illustrate that you should go out and pick up married women. It is simply to illustrate that there are a lot of men who are lousy, thoughtless lovers.

If only she could have all that she needs.

Imagine if she could meet a man who met all of her needs, a man who made her feel appreciated, who evokes a deep powerful emotional connection with her, makes her feel feminine and womanly and sexy, a man who gives her hot passionate sex. It's the kind of thing women dream about.

Through her life experiences, she begins to understand what she must have in a man. Some look for it in handsome men, some in popular men. She must have that feeling, but through a process of trial and error, including disappointment and despair, she begins to understand what she doesn't want in a man, like that guy who cheated on her or that guy who was too much of a marshmallow.

If she meets a man who is exciting, she finds that he is reckless; so she looks for a man who is considerate, but he becomes boring; so she goes with a man who is macho, but he ends up being uninteresting; so she seeks a man who is intelligent, but he is sexually bland; so she takes a man who is dominant, but he is in every way demanding.

If she could only meet a man who had all the things that could make her feel what she needed to feel—a man who is exciting without being reckless, considerate without being boring, macho without being uninteresting, intelligent without being bland, and dominant without being demanding.

That sounds like a contradiction, but it's not. A man does not have to be reckless to be exciting, and he does not have to be boring to be considerate. Most men don't understand that, which is why women say....

A good man is hard to find.

So, when I talk to women, they light up when I talk about this. I'll say, "I have asked women what they look for in a man, and what they tell me is..." (I hold my left hand out to the side.) "On the one hand, they find a man who is exciting, but he is reckless and inconsiderate." (I hold my right hand out to the side.) "And on the other hand, they find a man who is considerate, but he is boring." (Then, I point both of my hands to myself.) "If there could be just one man who has both, who is exciting AND considerate." They love that, and it all gets linked to me!

It is obvious why it is important that all four things be there. A woman is most fulfilled when she is with a man that she has everything with, but here is the extremely important aspect of all four things being there:

WHEN ALL FOUR THINGS ARE THERE, EACH THING BECOMES EVEN MORE POWERFUL

That is when she is with a man that she is wildly crazy about. That is when she can allow herself to become completely naked to him in every way. That is the pinnacle. That is when she is with a Masterful Lover.

CHAPTER 7
WOMEN'S DARK SECRET

"Women react to me the way that they do, Don Ottavio, because they sense that I search out the beauty that wells within them until it overwhelms everything, and then they cannot avoid their desires to release that beauty and envelope me in it."
~Don Juan DeMarco

As has been pointed out, women live a life of dichotomies. In fact, women need dichotomy in their lives in order to get everything they want.

THE DICHOTOMIES OF WOMEN

She wants to be appreciated and proper, but she also wants to be ruthlessly sexual.

A woman wants to be known by the people in her life as being innocent, but with her man, she wants to be naughty.

During the day, she is a proper, educated, professional woman with a career, but at night, in the bedroom, she wants to express her sexuality like a slut (without being a slut—a Big difference.)

During the day, she wants to be in control of her life and her destiny, but at night, in the bedroom, she wants to be submissive and told what she will do sexually.

Women don't want to be seen as sluts, but in the context of sexual intimacy with the man they trust, they love to be slutty.

In her everyday life, a woman does not like to be told what to do. But in the context of sexuality with the man she trusts, she responds very powerfully to being told exactly what to do.

During the week, she is very responsible, but on the weekends with her man, in the context of sexuality, she wants to be totally without responsibility.

Women are repulsed when strange men send her pictures of their erect penis, but in the context of sexual intimacy, they find it a huge turn-on when their man gets an erection.

Women are repulsed when strange men masturbate while fantasizing about her, but she finds it very exciting when her man masturbates while fantasizing about her.

On Sunday mornings, she is a Sunday school teacher. On Saturday nights, she gets slutty.

Women do not like it when men are possessive in a relationship, but in the context of sexuality, she loves to be "owned."

Women do not want to be objectified, but in the context of sexuality with her trusted lover, she loves to be treated like a piece of property.

Women are repulsed by the idea of being sexual with their father, but in the context of sexuality, she loves to call her lover "Daddy."

IN THE CONTEXT OF HEIGHTENED SEXUAL AROUSAL, <u>EVERYTHING</u> CHANGES

Certainly, every woman is different. Each woman has preferences, norms, and extremes unique to her.

THE DICHOTOMIES IN HER MAN

A woman is attracted to the dichotomy in her man. Her man must be sensitive, yet strong; caring, yet dominant; sweet, yet able to tell her what she will do sexually.

A woman is attracted to a man who is serious and focused about his career during the day, but who at night can be light-hearted and people-oriented.

A woman is attracted to a man who is confident (not cocky – big difference), but who also does not take himself too seriously.

In the living room, a woman expects her man to use proper anatomical terms, like penis and vagina. In the bedroom, she expects him to use slang terms, like cock and pussy. If he uses slang in the living room, she sees him as inappropriate. If he uses proper terms in the bedroom, she just laughs.

All of the above assumes a mentally healthy woman with a good sense of deservedness. It is true that there are mentally screwed up women with a bad sense of deservedness, and practicing the above is more of an affirmation to her, rather than a healthy expression of her sexuality (very big difference).

Another thing... Some men blame society, religion, or strict upbringings for repressing female sexual expressiveness. We know very well that women don't want to be sluts, but the reality is that they get slutty for us all the time. We hear women say they would never do a one-night stand, but the reality is that they do.

Society does not impose anything upon women, at least in Western cultures. Women choose it that way themselves. Women are social creatures. They want all that the social establishments have to offer. If there weren't a societal structure, women would create one.

Women are social creatures. They prefer it that way. They want to know if the man is a social creature. They want to know if he can work within the social rules. They will run him through all their social tests, and when he passes, they fuck him silly. It's simple really.

Women will continue to sustain the social norms and enjoy being on the arm of a proper gentleman, and women will continue to surrender when their man fucks them hard like the very naughty sluts that they love to be. Stop worrying about society, religion, or strict upbringings; instead, embrace the dichotomy of womankind.

Here is a letter from Jean in Maryland:

```
Dear David,

    I   read   your   book   "Secrets   of   Female
Sexuality"  last  evening  and  I  can't  thank
```

you enough for the valuable information. It just blew me away... finally someone understood me.

I am a very successful business women, and have many people (mostly men) working for me. I am in complete control, and I like that position, yet I have never understood why in other situations I don't want the control, I want to be led.

It finally became clear to me from the book that in an intimate relationship I want to be a WOMAN, and I want my partner to be the MAN. I don't want to make the dinner or date plans, I want him to, it shows that I am desirable, that I am a WOMAN (love that the most), and that he respects me. In a way I want to be taken care of, I want to be nurtured.

Also you said women need to be supported, so true, and we DO NOT want men to solve our problems, we really just need to emote, and have it accepted without judgment, just supported and admired. We can figure out the rest, we're pretty smart creatures.

I had all of this recently with a man that I had started dating, and I was so surprised how sensual and sexual I was becoming / feeling. Our dirty talk was more via emails, and I saw it as "foreplay" and I was always ready for sex. I couldn't understand how I could have an orgasm with him just playing with my tits, always had found it boring before! Then he must have found either my G-spot or my deep spot, but almost instantly, my first real vaginal orgasm. Now I can just think about it without even touching myself I have an orgasm.

I was actually beginning to think I was becoming addicted to sex or to him, and it really scared me! I don't want to lose myself in a man, so I wasn't sure if I had a problem, if I needed therapy, maybe an intervention! Certainly this was not something I thought I could discuss with a girlfriend, what would they think, that yes I did need that intervention!

Recently we have had outside problems unrelated to our relationship, but both of us have somewhat pulled away from each other. Because of this I don't feel the appreciation I did, I don't feel the unconditional love (allowing me to emote, and him not trying to solve the problem), and the sex has completely changed. I no longer feel anything when he touches my breasts, I now see him as selfish in the bedroom, when before all I wanted to do was please him sexually. I tried to explain that our sex was beginning to make me feel like a whore, I didn't feel good about myself when I was with him. He was completely confused, how could he not be confused, and I couldn't really explain it to him, I didn't even get it myself at the time.

So I think it all goes back to the very beginning:

1. A Woman wants to be with a man who makes her feel good about herself when she is with him.

2. We need to be respected, and yet feel desired, sexy, and always ready to be taken! (Oh god how I want to be taken!!!)

3. We need to feel as if we are being heard, and then usually we don't really have much we DO need to say... again respect and unconditional love / acceptance.

4. And most importantly, everyone needs to understand that Women want to be Women and treated like a Woman, and we want Men to be Men, and we will treat them like a MAN. A WOMAN wants to be both WOMAN, that responsible independent business women, and also that slut who craves sex anywhere, anytime, and in anyway that our MAN wants, or even better... directs it.

We women have had just as difficult a time understanding our roles in this every changing society as men have had accepting us becoming their equals. Yes, you are right that we want our men to be dominant in the bedroom, but also, to some degree, we want their domination in many other aspects of our relationship. We want doors opened for us, we want dates planned for us, we would love it if a man would plan the romantic vacation, instead of us, etc.

We can share equally the responsibilities on other issues such as what house to buy, how to raise the children etc., but please, let us be WOMEN and feel like WOMEN in our personal relationships. We will only, and CAN ONLY be a WOMAN if he is the MAN. Then he will start to understand the true magic of all of this, that as we feel more like a WOMAN he feels so much more as a MAN! What man wouldn't love that? It's a WIN WIN situation!

David, thank you again for the information in this enlightening book. I am so glad to finally understand myself, and know that I am truly normal!

My only question is: How do we delicately suggest this book to the man in our lives, without him feeling insecure about himself, wondering about his "performance" or lack there of? I truly believe this book is the key to a successful loving partnership. If everyone out there would read this book, all the therapists would go out of business; no one would need them anymore.

This should be a mandatory read for both Women and the Men we so dearly love and appreciate when they are being MEN and allowing us to be WOMEN!

Sincerely,

Jean from Maryland

CHAPTER 8
WHY WOMEN CRAVE ROMANCE

"Do you think this bed, these sheets, and such a corset can deliver your soul from the seductive dreams which you fear?"
~Giacomo Casanova

While men look at porn, women read 400-page romance novels. Romance novels are the sexual entertainment for women. It is all about emotions and shared experiences. It gives them the chance to vicariously live the life they really want to live.

The people who understand the love affair that women have with romance are the authors of romance novels. Nineteen leading romance novel authors contributed to a book called *"Dangerous Men and Adventurous Women,"* edited by Jayne Ann Krentz, University of Pennsylvania Press, 1992. It is a collection of essays describing the appeal of the romance novel.

It is fascinating and very enlightening.

Romance novels account for half of all book sales. Because women love them so much, I was curious about two things: what do women find so fascinating in the men featured in the books, and what is the psyche of the women readers?

This book would lead me to believe that what women admire in themselves is courage. Both of these manifest themselves, or are played out, in her making a dangerous man fall in love with her.

The Plot: Victory for her is in teaching him to love. "Heroes who are gentled by love yet who lose none of their warrior qualities in the process, and heroines who conquer devils without sacrificing their femininity."

"It requires that the hero acknowledge the heroine's heroic qualities in both masculine and feminine terms. He must recognize and admire her sense of honor, courage, and determination, as well as her traditionally female qualities of gentleness and compassion."

"It also requires a sexual bonding that transcends the physical, a bond that reader and writer know can never be broken."

The Romantic Hero: A warrior to be tamed. The romantic hero is a leader—strong intelligent, untamed, tough, courageous, cynical, macho and dangerous. Yet, he is communicative and, deep down, is susceptible to succumbing to the vulnerabilities of deep love.

The Romantic Heroine: A woman of courage. The romantic heroine is a woman of intelligence, integrity, loyalty, faith, confidence, but above all courage. She conquers every challenge, the most difficult of which is taming the hero.

Sex in the Romance Novel: Sex is a celebration of the bond created between the heroine and the hero.

"He also happens to be wonderful in bed. It is a given that a woman is entitled to sexual satisfaction and that a real man can't be fulfilled unless his partner is also fulfilled."

The Female Reader's Psyche: Learning to love one's self. In reading the romance novel, the woman escapes into a fantasy world where she can be everything she has always wanted to be and feel everything she has always wanted to feel with the security of knowing that there will be a happy ending.

"If the romance novel teaches a woman to love anybody, the person she must learn to love is herself."

CHAPTER 9
WOMEN AND THEIR FANTASIES

*"Do I want to be gang-banged? No.
Have I fantasized about it? Yes."*
~Monica

While she was growing up and learning what it means to be female, she developed elaborate sexual fantasies. Early fantasies often begin as crushes. Typically, she concentrated her romantic hopes and dreams on a movie star who she will never actually meet. In this context, she can imagine being in love without the complications of reality. It gives her mental practice at being desired, valued, and appreciated. As she matures, the fantasies became highly sexual, often being very involved and complicated with entire story plot lines.

The classic reference on the subject is *"My Secret Garden"* by Nancy Friday.

Friday interviewed hundreds of women and documented in intricate detail all the fantasies. It is fascinating and very eye opening. Most men will be surprised by how extremely sexual women are and how bizarre the fantasies can be. Many of the fantasies are of "being taken without objection," which would be interpreted in a court of law as rape.

Another excellent resource is *"Private Thoughts"* by Wendy Maltz and Suzie Boss.

This book is outstanding. It actually presents a thesis on the why and how of female fantasies. It explains many things about the female psyche.

The two main things I learned from the book are: 1. There is always a reason for a fantasy. Sometimes, it is obvious; sometimes it is deeply hidden. 2. There is a lot of good self-talk out there, and there is a lot of bad self-talk out there.

Maltz wrote that a woman's fantasy life is often a reflection of her search for sexual power, pleasure, and identity that started in childhood.

Maltz categorized scripted fantasies according to six different roles: Pretty Maiden, Victim, Wild Woman, Dominatrix, Beloved, and Voyeur.

Maltz wrote the following:

"Sexual fantasies often begin in childhood with romantic or sensual ideas that become sexual as girls mature. Through fantasy, children create a very private, inner playground. It's a perfect place for girls to develop and explore all sorts of new ideas, including their private sexual thoughts."

"Fantasies help us by enhancing self esteem and attractiveness, increasing sexual interest and desire, facilitating orgasm, celebrating the present, satisfying curiosity, rehearsing future possibilities, releasing stress and tension, preserving a pleasant memory, and coping with past hurts."

Since she was a little girl, a woman has been developing and exploring her sexuality and what it means to be a woman. She has been practicing how to use her beauty and charm to make a strong man fall in love with her.

Women grew up dreaming about being admired, about being seduced, and about surrendering to her man.

For women, sex is often about surrendering. She can only be ruthlessly expressive when she has no responsibility for the act. When she is "taken" and "ravished," she can be ruthless.

Taken to an extreme, it explains the popularity of the rape fantasy, as shown in "*My Secret Garden*." No woman wants to be raped, but many women have masturbated to the fantasy of being raped, of being so desired, that a man would do anything to be with her, to ravish her, to fuck her hard. In this particular fantasy context, she can be as ruthless as possible, and she doesn't have to take any responsibility for it.

CHAPTER 10

WOMEN WANT MEN TO KNOW THIS

"I was quite surprised to discover how quickly my body responded to being touched in the right way. When a man knows how to make love to a woman, it changes everything."
~Kim Cattrall

Women will make the investment to learn what they can to make sex better, and they are very frustrated when their man is not willing to do the same. Here is an e-mail from Marian:

Hello David,

I came across your book through my brother. I feel like I am more curious and interested in finding out how to please my boyfriend more than he is. It seems like this book is for guys who are looking for more ways to be sexually creative with women, not the other way around, and I'm wondering if I will benefit from it.

To give you a brief understanding, my boyfriend is my first. He's 6 years older and sometimes thinks he knows everything.

I like going on the net and finding new things out about anything that interests me (sex being one of them). I don't have a lot of experience with it so I guess I like going and finding out how to please the guy in different ways, techniques, whatever. He just looks down on this kind of thing.

I would be so pleased if he was equally interested, so that it would become a joint venture that would bring our intimacy closer.

I don't expect him to change and I'm not trying to make him change. I just want to change and improve myself as a woman, a human being, a friend. I just want to be the best I can be.

Women don't even know how to teach a man. Here is an e-mail from Kayla:

Hi David!

I'm not completely sure if this is going to be a question you can answer, but after reading your e-mails I can't stop thinking about it.

I happen to fall into the category of women who have never had an orgasm, and knowing that there are guys (Masterful Lovers) out there that can make that happen is both encouraging and depressing. Why don't they find me?

How can I find a masterful lover?

I have met a variety of men. I went through the bad boy stage and now I'm looking more for respect and trust.

What I seem to find are men that I have to sort of "teach", in a way, how to please me (in which I don't even really know).

I guess I like the sexual intentions of the guys I meet because I like to be sexual more often than not, but they often lack the communication skills that I need and the ability to be in control. They always want me to take charge, but I won't do that until I am FULLY comfortable. They don't understand that.

Here is an e-mail from Christina:

Hi David,

My name is Christina. I'm desperate for your advice. Please help me if you can.

I've written to you before asking for pointers on how I can please my boyfriend.

In the message I told you that I've never orgasmed before, not even with him, but that I wasn't so concerned with that as much as his pleasure.

Now... I'm more concerned about my own. I read your newsletters religiously and after every one I read I'm so jealous of all of these women who have these amazing orgasms that it almost brings me to tears.

Well now it has.

I thought I'd convinced him to order your book. But he hasn't. I try not to bring up the fact that I never orgasm to him because I don't want him to feel worse than he already does for not being capable.

He wants to give me orgasms, he really does, but he keeps saying (when I do bring it up) that it's something I have to do.

He asks me if something happened in my childhood that would prevent me from letting go with him, since sometimes I say in bed, "I can't" and push him away.

First of all nothing happened in my childhood that prevent this. No rape. Nothing.

Secondly I've said that in the past because yes, the feeling was so intense I felt like I couldn't take it. Other times it's just because what he's doing kinda hurts or just doesn't feel good at all. But the past several times we've had sex I've not stopped him at all. Trying to 'let go' and nothing has happened. I don't know what to do anymore.

I don't know how to get him to buy your book. I've forwarded your newsletters to him. I've asked him a few times too.

I DON'T KNOW WHAT ELSE TO DO.

He thinks it's something that I have to do, like I said. He asks me what he needs to do. I can't even give myself an orgasm, how am I supposed to show him how to do it?

Our sex, other than my not having an orgasm, is great. We talk dirty in bed, share our kinky fantasies, have sexy text messages, but I'm never satisfied in the end.

Is there any advice you have for me? I'm desperate. He's about to propose and I'm scared that I will be stuck with never having one. Please help if you can.

Thank you.

Women are frustrated that men won't study up. Here is an e-mail from Cindy:

David,

I am a woman who finally has discovered her inner sexual being.

I have been getting your newsletters for several months now and enjoy reading them. They are geared mostly toward men and how they can help their woman.

One problem I've ran across with my "newfound" abilities, is that being a giver I find men get "addicted" to a mind-blowing bj and then forget about me. I have had men tell me no woman has ever done to them what

I have. It is great to know you can please someone to that extent.

Anyway, my question for you is: Is there any way I can use your book to help myself achieve things in a relationship where you know your partner would never even consider reading the book?

Here is an email from Mary:

Hi David,

My husband does not please me sexually. I have told him that this is a big problem for me and I really want to explore my sexuality with him. I gave him an ultimatum and we are now in counseling.

I signed him up for your newsletter and it seemed good for a while. He was taking more time with me in the bedroom and tried to find my deep spot. Well, I'm a sexual person and can bring myself to orgasm, but I am not that comfortable with him. I need to really feel like he wants me and wants to explore me and accepts me.

After 12 years together with him getting his pleasure and then going to sleep without any attention paid to my pleasure, it takes me a while to warm up. I sometimes feel insecure that it can take me a while to come, but that is only with him. When I am alone, it is not a problem. And I imagine that if I were with another man who was interested in my pleasure, the fact that it might take 20 minutes to 40 minutes of sexual play to get me over the edge would be seen more as fun than a chore.

I thought we were getting somewhere but he seems to have given up and gone back to old habits.

We have a wonderful life together otherwise. Great kids, good jobs, great friends, etc., but I don't want to live the rest of my life not feeling desired and fulfilled. Not feeling like I'm worth the time and effort to have a fulfilling sex life. I am so conflicted because it seems like a petty reason to leave a good man (sex isn't everything) but, it would be my reason. I have to make a decision about being with him. I do not want to continue in limbo. Either he will learn to satisfy me, or I will find someone else, but it is not fair to me to sacrifice my sexual side, and it is not fair to him for me to cheat. And I have to admit, that is a huge temptation for me.

I am happy to try any new thing that might help. He is satisfied. I do any position he wants and blow jobs, etc. I email him sexy pictures, etc.

I masturbate regularly, but I want my man to give me orgasms.

Also, another last thing. I have told him many many times that it hurts for him to go too deep. He hits my cervix and it causes extreme. And yet, he still does this. Does he really have that little self control or does he just not care or understand how painful this is?

I appreciate any advice you have.

Thank you,

Mary

CHAPTER 11

WHY WOMEN WANT TO BE LED

*"If control was out of my hands, I, in turn,
was allowed to be out of control."*
~Elizabeth McNeill

Women grew up in the social conditioning that it is feminine and proper to be sexually submissive and that it is unacceptable to be sexually forward. Because she is sexually submissive, she can only enjoy sexuality when she cannot be blamed for it. By following the lead of her man, she can be "slutty" without "being a slut." Only when her man assumes the responsibility for what happens can she be fully sexually expressive.

Here is an e-mail from Melinda:

```
Dear David

I was wondering what would be the best way
to tell my boyfriend that I would like to be
spanked while he is fucking me... or maybe
even tied to the bed and "forced" to be
submissive. I am not sure how to bring this
up without him thinking that I am a freak.
```

Most women are sexually submissive. In the bedroom, they actually like to be told what to do. However, being submissive causes a dichotomy. How can she tell her man what she wants him to make her do if she is by definition submissive?

Women want a confident man who will lead. If men only knew how to lead. If men only knew that women want them to lead. Here is an e-mail from Cathy:

I appreciate the message that you are providing men, "Be the Man, be confident, lead her, etc." I wish that men could get their heads wrapped around the fact that they really could have anything they wanted if they simply knew the correct approach.

Here is an e-mail from Debbie:

I need your help in figuring this out! What is my problem?

My husband is a good lover. He wants to give me sex that I enjoy. I am so fortunate with him. I really do love my life, but then there is sex... we only have sex 3-4 times a week. I can't seem to get enough. I seem to want to do it all the time. I don't want to stop wanting it either.

Outside of the bedroom, and in social interactions, I'm "politeness and manners." But as I look around, I find that I am attracted to the same type of man, confident air, nice form, striking eyes, nice butt, and outgoing and aggressive. And my husband is a handsome nice guy, very polite, loving, well groomed, considerate, generous, caring, benevolent.

I love being treated like a lady, in the living room and in public, but I really do want to be ravished and ravish someone in the bedroom.

I always attract this type of man, and there is nothing wrong with them. Why isn't this enough for me? I simply feel that something is missing, so I guess I am looking. I must still be wanting. It's like I am always ready. Sometimes I feel as though I can't look at men for too long, or I could take someone up on their offer...

worse yet. I can simply cum if I am staring too long!

I imagine sex to be awesome with someone dominant, talking dirty to me, making me do things beyond by inhibitions. I would love it. Just thinking about this makes me feel sexual, extremely excited. I don't know what it is! How can I attract or get what I want?

My husband constantly draws me in by being sweet and gentlemanly. I'm drawn to his masculine confidence, we make love, but then I am totally charged for some raw sex.

Sometimes I don't think that I am a very good person. I enjoy really exciting sex, I like being secretive, but I have no intentions of relinquishing anything that I have for anyone else.

In college I would go out and look for "Badboys", but they were a great deal of trouble. The sex was awesome. Will I always crave those intense sexual feelings?

What the hell is wrong with me?

In fact, sometimes women want their man to get rough. Here is an e-mail from Jenny:

Hi David,

I don't mind aggression when making love. Sometimes it really turns me on.

My man is an amazing lover. It's in the way he takes control of my body. He pulls and moves my body aggressively in different positions. It shows that he wants to give me sex that I enjoy. He would massage my vagina with his fingers very intensely. It's wonderful, even better than when he uses his penis.

I love it.

At the moment I can't seem to get enough. I just seem to want to do it all the time. I don't want to stop wanting it either.

Women want their man to at least start something. Here is a post to Craigslist.org from Feb 3, 2008.

Just fucking fuck me, already.

Dear Men of Craigslist,

Look, I know you men have it difficult. Women are just about impossible to understand, much less please. In a post-feminist society, you never know exactly what you should be doing. Women are bloody picky, I know we are. It can be scary, too, when women freak out about what appear to be benign issues. And men who do their best to be respectful, female-positive humans, I salute you, I do.

But please, please just fuck me already. Honestly, I appreciate your thoughtfulness. I like that you want to take things slow. I can totally get behind the idea of emotional connection, but dearjesusinheaven, FUCK ME. We've done dinner and drinks. We've gone dancing. We've cuddled and watched a movie. I'm wearing a low cut shirt and you've been staring at my breasts all night. Goodgodalmighty, get to it and fuck me.

When we get hot and heavy, please take charge. Please, please fuck me. Trust me, I'm not going to just lie still–I'll get involved. But don't make me force your hand into my panties. That makes me feel like a rapist. We've been kissing for a half hour and your hand keeps grazing my ass. That's nice, but it's time to move forward. Get on top of me. Don't make me get on top right out of the gate and start bobbing up and down on your cock like I'm practicing some crazy new aerobic yoga because YOU won't go down on me. Roll on top and start dry humping like a good boy should. Don't gently suck my nipples and then pull back when I moan with pleasure. You being coy is totally not what I want. It's not what WE want.

OK, I know it's scary. There are lots of women out there who make fucking really difficult. So, I have compiled some handy tips. Don't think of this as complaining, or as schadenfreude for the Andrea Dworkins of the world. Just some simple tips, for timid men who have forgotten what it means to fuck like men:

1. Taking charge is not bad. Oh, there will be some women who feel that you are pushy. If you are making out with a woman, and she starts to push back, ask nicely if things are moving too fast. If she says yes, say something like "I'm sorry - you just look so fucking delicious. I'll go slower." Otherwise, skillfully move forward. If you start kissing a woman, and she responds well, and before long, you're both on the floor with her skirt pushed up, and you on top of her, it's not the time to roll onto your back and start awkwardly stroking the top of her head. Seriously, grow a goddamn pair. YOU'RE the man. Act like one.

2. Ohmyfuckinggod, please learn to respect the clit. It's different for every woman, so ask what she likes. Do not, I repeat, do not just wiggle your fingers around her pussy like you're trying to tickle her. Do not drum your fingertips against her vulva like you are impatiently waiting at the Sears Tire Center for your receipt. Do not push the clit like it is a doorbell at

some house that you need to get inside of. Start by using all four fingers with firm yet gentle pressure against the outside of her pussy. Do not charge in with a single finger and start jabbing at things. And if you really don't know what to do, ask her. Just ask. "How do you like it?". It's a simple question, and most women will answer straight out. If she's being all coy, ask "Do you like pressure? Is it sensitive?" The clitoris is a varied item, indeed. Treat each one as though you have never encountered one before. Forget everything that your last partner liked.

3. Most women like to be fucked, and fucked well. Yes, there are women out there who want to "make love" every time - sweet, gentle, rocking love with lots of eye contact and loving kisses. Those women are not the majority. The majority like to be pounded. The majority like to have their hair pulled. The majority like a good, solid jackhammering. When a woman is bucking wildly against you, it's not because she wants you to pull back and slowly swirl your cock around her vagina like you're mixing a cake batter up there. It's because she wants you to hold down her arms, or grab her hips, or push her legs above her head, and fuck her harder. Don't be too afraid of what this means as far as gender equality goes - I am a raging feminist bitch, but I still want to be penetrated like you are planning on fucking my throat from the inside out.

4. A little roughness is nice. Do not pretend that you had no idea that some women like their hair pulled. Do not act shocked if she wants you to spank her ("Really?

Spanking? Won't it hurt?" - yes, it does. That's the fucking point). We know you've read Stuff and Maxim, and that's all those laddie mags talk about in their "How to Please Her" sections. Start with light, full handed smacks to the area of her ass that she sits on. Judge her response and continue on from there. You don't have to bend her over one knee and tell her she's a naughty girl and that Daddy's going to punish her; save that for the fifth date. Women are less delicate than you think, so don't worry about breaking her hip.

5. It's OK for you to make noise. Otherwise, we feel like we are fucking a ninja. Unless you actually are a ninja, and have sneaked into our rooms with vibrating nanuchaku and zippered black pajamas, please, please make some noise. If you're banging a woman, and she's crying out and saying your name and moaning, and you can't even manage a grunt, she's going to feel like an idiot. You don't have to make the sounds she is making, but do SOMETHING. You know how when you are watching porn, and the girl does something great to the guy and the guy kind of goes "Ah!", half grunt, half yell? That's HOT. Do that. Whisper our name (assuming you know it) gruffly. Groan against her neck when you're in missionary position. You don't have to grunt like a mountain gorilla, but if you are totally mute, she's going to get worried.

6. Most women like dirty talk, in addition to the grunting. If you'd like to get some dirty talk going, ask her if she likes the way you fuck her. If she responds well, continue with something like, "I love fucking you. God, you look so fucking

hot." Is she still moaning in response? "Your tits are so beautiful." Does that work? If she doesn't respond well to the term "tits", you might have to stop there. If she keep moaning or responding, pass Go and collect $200. Try the following:

"Oh, god. Your pussy is SO tight."

"You're so wet - are you wet because you like the feel of my cock ramming you?"

"I think I'm going to come inside you. I'm going to fill up your little cunt." It doesn't matter that you're wearing a condom; we LOVE hearing this.

If all of those work, you can then progress to things like "sexy little bitch" and "dirty whore". Tread carefully, but please, tread. Do not tiptoe. Do not sit down. Charge.

6. You're not obligated to eat a woman out. In return, she's not obligated to choke on your dick. Don't skip one and expect the other. If you do eat a woman out, the only comment you should make about her pussy is how nice it is. The length of her labia minora, the color of her interior, her waxing job or full bush - you are not John Madden. No time for color commentary.

7. Do not bitch about condoms. Oh, we hate them. Trust us. They hurt us more than they hurt you. But we don't want to be preggers, and you don't want to catch anything, right? Don't whine about condom sex. Do not explain that you can't come with one on. LEARN to come with one on, or if not, help us figure out what to do with you once we're satisfied and it's time for you to let loose your load.

8. We really like it when you come. It's called a money shot for a reason. Watching semen shoot out of you is one of the most gratifying things EVER. However, do not assume that she wants you to jack it off onto her face. She might, but don't assume. Seeing and/or feeling you come is rewarding for us, so there's no need to deprive us of it, but please do consult us before unleashing. "I think I'm going to come - how do you like it?" is a fair question that shouldn't rob you of your testicles.

In recent memory, I've been fucked by a very aggressive, manly guy, and I've been... well, fucked is the wrong term here. I've been penetrated by a total and utter wuss. Who am I going to run back to when I'm ready for my fill? Manly McHardon, that's who.

*New point of clarification - some people have brought up some really great issues in response to this post, so let me say this: I don't mean to imply that all women like to be treated like whores. I do mean to say that most women I know have told me that they like sex rougher than most men give it to them. Rough does NOT equal chains and bondage. And this applies to the bedroom only, and does not mean that she wants you to choose her dinner for her, or treat her like less of a person. **Some women have said that they don't like it rough and what the hell am I thinking? Well, girls, you're in the minority. HOWEVER, all women need to remember that, in addition to be straight forward about your sexual desires, you need to be straight forward about your sexual limits. Don't be afraid to ask for more, but when something feels wrong, say so. Don't ever do something you don't want to do in silence and then blame the guy. Silence is dangerous.

Some women would be happy if their man would just do something. Here is an e-mail from Denise:

Hi David,

As a woman, let me first say how right you are about us. We want to be respected in the living room, but "taken" and dominated in the bedroom. Never thought any man would figure that out.

Here's my question. I've been with my man for 20 years. We have a great relationship, but we have one problem... I want sex every single day and I want hot, steamy, slutty sex. He doesn't seem to. Is it that it is not "normal for me"? Out of character...

I should say that while I had secret sex fantasies all along, I never spoke them out loud to him until now. I wanted to reconnect, I thought more exciting sex was the answer, but it's seemed to turn him off. I've basically been speaking every sexual thought to him recently. I thought this would excite him... but no, or so it seems.

He looks at porn EVERY day on the internet, so it's not for a lack of interest in my opinion, but he rarely initiates sex with me. As I stated before I want to be taken/dominated... thus waiting for him to make the first move - engage in sex. How can I get him to know this? Is there any hope for this relationship to continue if sex is not part of the deal? The kind of sex I want? I recently showed him my deep spot (btw, thanks - didn't know it was there until I started reading your newsletters), I've guided him to my g-spot - he thought it was a myth... what more can I do?

Is it possible for a man to think of his best friend, wife, mother of his children as a bedroom slut waiting to be banged over and over? I am an attractive 40 year old, thin, other men find me sexually desirable - I know because I've been propositioned many times over - so what's wrong with me????

Please help me. Thanks much. -desperate housewife wanting her man the way it should be!

Leading can be a difficult thing for men to do, but when they get some courage, they are very pleased with the results. Here is an e-mail from Anthony in Massachusetts:

You say it again and again, "Women crave to find a strong, dominant, powerful man." It might sound like a cliché, but it's totally true.

I remember the first time I told a woman exactly what I wanted her to do. It felt a little scary, but I told her exactly what to do, feel, think, -- everything.... She LOVED every second of it, and later, as she basked in the glow of being fucked beyond her wildest dreams, she asked me how I became such an incredible lover.

On that night something shifted in me. I realized that I could please any woman if I chose to. Ultimately it led to a greater appreciation of my manliness. Now I choose the women I please carefully. The off-balance urgency is gone. I've realized that being a strong, dominant male isn't about what you do, it's about who you are.

Thank you, David for helping me on the path to discovering myself.

Anthony

CHAPTER 12
WHAT WOMEN ARE PISSED OFF ABOUT

"There are some things a man can never recover from."
~Mark Cunningham

I receive emails from frustrated women on a daily basis. As always, the names have been changed to protect the not so innocent.

Here is an e-mail from Olivia:

David,

I have hesitated writing this, but it has been on my mind for the past three days. I stumbled upon your Master Lover website merely by accident. I have to say, I found the deep spot video instead of something else, but when I played it, my first reaction was – this has got to be the most elaborate hoax I have ever seen in my life. This guy David Shade must be a sadistic sex maniac leading men into yet another porno-mentality website. But then I really got into all the other links and realized you were on the level. In a word, I was at first stunned that at least one man had the gall and fortitude to find out what women want and desire. You really DID do your homework!

I am a 50 plus female, and sad to say I fall into the category of disillusioned and unsatisfied sexually my whole life with men. I am totally heterosexual with a strong sex drive that drove me to start masturbating at the age of twelve. I am highly orgasmic, but never had one in intercourse and no man has ever given one to me - or really cared enough to try.

I have had only six male partners in my lifetime; all who were as you called "lame" lovers. I was married for twenty years to a man who used my vagina to masturbate in. Sex to him was, kiss and drool while shoving his tongue into my mouth, tweak my nipples a couple of times, maybe massage my clitoris for three minutes, and then when I was 'ready and wet' slammed it home.

I tried everything to tell him what I liked, bought books, videos - you name it, I attempted to educate him, but he was clearly not interested. Like women say, all the materials are out there - but men do not read them - WOMEN DO! I do not know why, unless they really do not care. My six experiences, all of them felt like they got theirs, I had to get mine - which I did on my own to keep from going insane with sexual frustration of agonizing engorgement in my vaginal regions when I was left out on the limb with no finish. I was not about to have sex with five thousand men to hopefully find the right one because I really am a one man woman. I give it all to my man. I really gave up entirely and prayed my hands never fall off.

But I have to say, you are 100% right about women and what they want. I never thought I'd say that to a MAN. I wish to god I could find a man to give me an orgasm... any kind of orgasm! I know I am multi-orgasmic from clitoral stimulation (3 is my lucky number) but it is not fulfilling all by yourself all the time your entire life. I have been divorced for the past ten years and not even dated - because I know I will hear the same old "I'll turn you into twins, you will cum like crazy with me" routine, and I will be laying there thinking "why did I do this to myself again and my cervix will be so inflamed, I wont be able to sit for a week?"

In my entire life, I almost had an orgasm from a man on two separate occasions. The first was my husband from oral stimulation, but just when I almost came, he decided I was 'wet enough for entry' which he felt oral sex for women was all about (naturally for him it was his birthright). He really was not that good at oral sex anyway, but I never had a chance.

The second time I almost had an orgasm from a man, I am sad to say came from a guy I cheated on husband with. My husband cheated on me for many years.

You are right that if women are not satisfied sexually, they will cheat. I never thought I would, and it took me 15 years of being tired of feeling treated like a human "cum bucket." I was desperate in trying to find THE ONE for me. Our marriage was stale and taking a nose dive and I did not love him anymore for the terrible way he treated me.

Well, one incident out of three years of cheating with this other man, one time during him giving me digital masturbation, I almost came until he suddenly asked me "You don't mind if I put the game on do you?" That was it for me - I was devastated. I kept trying with this guy, but he turned out to be lame too so I dumped him too.

WHY are men like this, David? Why are most of them so wrapped up in their own members and they really do not care? They pretend to care to get you in the mood, but the proof was in the pudding - only done for selfish reasons. And all my girlfriends, married and single say the same thing. Do men feel it doesn't matter, women will let them use our bodies anyway so why bother? I would love to know why men are like this - or the bad ones. I commend the men who come here trying to please women; I find it most shocking that some out there actually care... but probably not enough of them do this - what a pity for the female sex.

It was shattering to me as a woman to be used as I was in my marriage and I decided to divorce my husband too. I have not been with a man since because I have felt so used by them, but yet I love men and desire so much to find a man that would be like the kind of men you have described. You are right on the money about women wanting the man to take the lead, to talk dirty, and most importantly to realize how much we want to have orgasms too! My god, every woman I know in my friendships over forty years have told me how unhappy they are, yet they still subject themselves to the crappy sex.

I just wanted to tell you, that I did try the deep spot on myself, purely out of curiosity. I think what it does is stimulate the inner muscles into involuntary spasms which deepen vaginal orgasms (I can have both kind with clitoral stimulation only and no penetration). I could not orgasm like that with just the finger insertion, it was too painful (and I know I did it correctly). But afterwards, during clitoral stimulation I had both types of orgasm happen – clitoral and vaginal at the same time and it was MIND BLOWING. I would LOVE for that to happen during intercourse. The vaginal portion of it was very intense and I made myself scream! LOL!

Like other women, we long to have orgasms during intercourse with our men, but I am not sure it would happen to me. But I am pretty much at a dead end in my life sexually anyway. I have been asked by so many people of why, because of how attractive, funny and smart I am, how is it that I do not have a man in my life or why did I not remarry. My story I just told is the reason why. I have been so disappointed, I do not want to have my hopes shattered again and be left frustrated for the latter portion of my life. After reading your blog, I think I will not go out with a man unless he is a graduate of your course. (GRIN)

I would love to know, as a woman, why no matter what the age category, most men are simply NOT interested in female sexuality, only concerned with their own pleasure. I say this not only from my own personal experience in life, but all of my various female friends of different ages from age groups of 20, 30 and 40 year olds. They are ALL frustrated, angry and fed up with the diet of the "intercourse is the be-all end-all" drummed into the female cranium since we are able to know what sex is. Maybe I can help them to understand if I can understand. I hope that you can get a large enough male membership so they finally wake up!

But anyway, I must commend you for what you have attempted to do. I think every man should at least read your website. I do not know what your materials contain, but I am sure they are worthy of high achievement. I am so sorry it took you to fall to your knees in your marriage, but look at you now! I bet your wife wish she had another chance!

Thank you for all your hard work! Great work David, I'd be very happy to see your response to my email.

I replied to Olivia with:

You have no idea how many emails I get like yours. I do not know what the hell is wrong with men that they would be so ignorant and thoughtless. I try to help men, but most just don't accept it.

I am glad you liked my video about the deep spot, and especially glad to hear that it resulted in your first vaginal orgasm!

I want to ask you about that. You said you tried the finger insertion but it was too painful. You can try a toy with a bent tip. That could be more comfortable. Take your time with it. Start gentle. Let yourself get used to the new stimulation.

Response from Olivia:

I thank you so much for your prompt response and I am very appreciative you took the time to write back.

I also thank you for trying to proffer some kind of reason to explain the sexual dilemma between men and woman. Of course I know that is virtually impossible to find one sole answer, but your response was very sincere and also accurate.

From a woman's perspective, I find it so sad that there is such a wedge between our genders physically, which ultimately deteriorates to such an extent that it affects us emotionally in a negative capacity. In my circumstance, and I know many other women, we love so completely and give so much of ourselves in relationships, if only we had a fraction of that in return from our guys – men would benefit from that immensely. I know you know that.

I have to tell you that without meeting you personally, you are one in a million and a very special man. I do not offer that compliment readily to the opposite sex, but any one who has been through the kind of pain you experienced, and rose above it and made your quest the one that it is right now, takes an incredible amount of reflective, self examination, courage, and caring. You genuinely think about not only women, but men too and the quality of their lives. You were fortunate enough to find the magic equation. I do hope that you are content now and have the kind of love you deserve!

Thanks for the tip on the toy, but I so wish it was a real live, wonderful man instead... maybe some day god might answer my prayers and I will not have to live my life out in loneliness.

As I said, keep up the good work and tell these guys the truth – pound it into their skulls if you must for maybe they will listen to YOU since you have such a professional manner and a very sharp intellect. Guys will listen to another man about sex before they will their own woman. Maybe you can help them to living better lives in their relationships, as you have with the ones who finally "got it!"

Take care and I will be visiting your website from time to time! It is a little difficult since it makes me sad to be on my side of the coin, but I am happy for those who are successful and are on the right track. I intend to tell my girlfriends to veer their men to your website so they might have a chance at happiness too.

Thanks so much, David!

Here is an e-mail from Kristen:

Hello, I feel lost. In every relationship I've ever been in I have always been the giver and very rarely if ever, see it returned equally. Always being thoughtful in letting them know that I care about them and that they are special to me and I show them how they are special to me in many ways. When we have problems and I don't know what to do. I seek help through friends, family, looking online. Any and all resources available to give me help. I do my best to leave drama out of the relationship and to calm down and think logically before talking to my man. Life creates drama all by itself so why add to it.

I find myself falling into the group of sexually unsatisfied women. When my boyfriend and I have sex he always finishes. Shortly afterward he is asleep. He stays awake for a little while and we cuddle and talk but he can't stay awake for long. I know and understand this is just the way guys are built but I find it very unfair that he has never tried to help me finish afterwards.

I have looked everywhere trying to find ways to solve this problem of me not finishing. I am always willing to try new things with my boyfriend and have told him this a few times. I always go into the bedroom with him with hope that this time we are going to find a way for both of us to enjoy sex fully and completely. I find it shocking that every time I have hope and still no improvement.

I am beginning to become very frustrated (in more than one way) and am starting to become bored and lose hope. This makes me very sad. I feel that my man and I have lots of potential and that we are great together, though with this problem at hand I feel our connection fading and my happiness in the relationship less and less. I feel that I have exhausted all other media for help.

Please PLEASE HELP!

Here is an e-mail from Karen:

Hi David, I'm Karen. I was so pleased when I found your website. I thought you are the answer of my problem. It's about my boyfriend.

We have been seeing each other for more than a year now. But I find our sex life is so boring. We normally have sex every Saturday night. Never had spontaneous sex or any unexpected one.

I am very giving. I give him blow jobs or whatever he requests. I find it very frustrating sometimes. I get paranoid and think that maybe he is not attracted in me.

His foreplay is very poor and I find it very hard. I love him but I am scared to tell him what or how I want our sex life will be. I don't want him to think anything dirty about me.

I am really confused now. Please advice.

Here is an e-mail from Marilyn:

Recently my best friend told me about you. As a result, I did a bit of research on the internet and ordered your "Secrets of..." book. I read through some of it but the reason I ordered it was to get my husband to read it and hopefully start him on a path of learning a little more about what I need to change in our relationship.

We have been married 5 years, and I am totally in love with him. He is a very good person who loves me dearly but is not only not adventurous in bed, he basically does the same thing every single time we are together and has no sense of what turns me on. I have talked to him about it many many times and I think he just doesn't know where to start. In the early days I was more inclined to "teach" him but I am sick of always being the teacher and of always being the aggressor. He is almost too respectful.

Much of what you talk about resonates with me but I have no idea where to start with this. He does not know how much this is bothering me. I do know he has read some of your book but I know it's been a few weeks now and other things have gotten in the way. We've had some very candid conversations about it this and has mostly happened when our sexual liaisons have ended with him coming and I've been left tied in knots with him not knowing what to do other than the SAME OLD SAME OLD which basically turns me off these days.

Really unsure of where to start and my friend said I should email you and perhaps you could give some guidance ??

I would really appreciate anything you could offer in terms of what direction I should take. I can hardly believe I've written any of this down to a total stranger but she has been my best friend for more than a lifetime now and I trust her dearly. She has highly recommended you.

Here is an e-mail from Audrey:

I love my boyfriend very much. He feels really great in bed... but even though we've discussed some sexual techniques, fantasies, etc. I believe he's all talk, and pretty much inexperienced (he comes from a male dominant family, tons of guy friends, few girl friends, and no one talks about sex it seems - unless it's porn talk).

My want with him sexually, is for him to get me to that point and help me over the top. I feel selfish and I am holding back a lot of what we can be doing together, because I WANT to come too. I worry that if I make sex as exciting as I really want it to be, he just won't be able to handle it. Okay, basically, I'm saying: while he can make me cum very nicely, it's a surprise for both of us, like a lucky session or something. He tries his best to hold on as long as he can, while I "take forever" in coming... and usually, I lose.

I ask for things and he acts squeamish or confused, or like it's just my body that isn't responding fast enough... but he does feel sorry and regretful that he "couldn't last".

He is inexperienced. I want him to know, hear, read, believe, that he needs to fuck my brains before he fucks my body, that it helps get me where we both want me to be. I want him to understand that his holding back on doing other things to please me sexually (i.e. oral, nipple stim, etc.) makes me feel unsexy, undesirable, not loved or respected enough to be worth the "effort".

My question is: Which book of yours should I buy that will help him learn this?

I love the guy - but I don't think I am capable of just loving him and being the hole he fills when the need arises (sense the frustration). I like feeling lucky... but I want to be lucky all the time.

I used to think love holds so much more value than sex, but I AM sexual and that little bit of feeling "left behind" is beginning to wear on me, and I can't stop my mind from believing that there is someone else who will love me AND naturally want to satisfy this basic need, as well.

Thanks so much for your wisdom. I am thrilled that you are spreading the word to these men. It's good to read that men are just as interested in pleasing a woman as they are in having their own great O. Though, I'm thinking you're teaching them, it goes hand in hand, so to speak.

(ego boost for man = happy woman = win!!)

I too wonder sometimes if you really are a woman, because you know SO much truth about us!

Here is an e-mail from Jenny:

I'm a woman of 36 years. Before I married my husband I could sometimes have an orgasm although usually I faked it. I've now been married for 10 yrs and the only time I have an orgasm is when I am alone and fantasize.

Of late my husband seems to be changing the approach by becoming so loving, but I can't respond because I just feel switched off.

At times, I'd rather watch porn which I don't want or like or just get a candle, cover it with a condom, and push it in just to have an orgasm, I don't like all this but I find myself doing it. Am I going mad or what? I am embarrassed to share this with anyone, maybe because it is such a strange thing.

Secondly, of late there has been this husband of my friend who I have talked with several times on a number of personal issues. He recently told me that he realized how much he loved me and how he hurt inside because he could not do anything about it considering the many obstacles ahead. I didn't like the idea at first and I told him that if he does not stop this I'd report him to my husband. He said he'd respect my views but that would not change his feelings about me which he has harbored inside him for 2 years.

My job involves being with this person in carrying out our day to day tasks. Amazingly, I've found myself developing a love passion inside of me and always yearning to be with him, although situations cannot allow it.

He told me he loved me not because of what he could do to/with me but because of who I am and that he'd ensure he does anything to make me happy and not to hurt me. I found myself telling him for the first time that I loved him too. Afterwards I rebuked myself for saying that even though I miss him so much when I am not with him.

My question is am I going mad with these sudden strange feelings or what? Is it normal for a woman of 36 years to behave like this? Why didn't I feel this way when I was younger? I'm a mother of 2 children but I still don't understand this. Please advise me out of this madness.

Here is an e-mail from Samantha:

I'm 44 yrs old, female and dying to find a man who can master this. In fact, I wanna know everything you teach but then what? I'd love to find a guy who's willing to learn these skills. How do I introduce a fella to this w/o wounding his ego? Do I buy the whole program and have it on hand?

I've tried in the past to explain some of this (I haven't read all your material yet) but some of this info is internal/ instinctual to us. We just know it but don't know how to explain it. I tried to explain - in the nicest possible way-getting the brain going, having a commanding presence, using great little dirty talk, exuding confidence and taking the lead. I think it intimidates them.

For example, I've tried to whisper in his ear, "It turns me on when you tell me what you wanna do to me." when things were getting cozy and intimate. The last man that I was involved with said he didn't wanna insult me. It's hard to insult me w/ your swinging richard in my mouth. He would use words like, "member" and "vagina". Please, this is not a lab or medical class. Nothing HOT about a "member".

If I hand your materials over to the next fella (the last one, "member" dude, disappeared by alien abduction), will I be insulting him or telling him he doesn't know what he's doing, "Here's an instruction book on what you think you're good at" or wounding his ego? I really am aware of the fragile male ego and try to tread lightly, but a girl wants to have fun, ya know? How do I get mankind in my small world on board w/ your program?

Here is an e-mail from Maggie:

Dear David,

I have been reading your e-mails for some time. I'm sure you can imagine that after 20 years I'm intrigued by the idea of new ideas to enhance our love for each other. I decided to just start forwarding my favorite emails to him and let him get the hint.

Well... he has not taken any action on them and I'm a little frustrated. He's my husband of 20 years and the father of our 2 children, so the idea of dumping him for someone who is willing to go farther to satisfy me, well, seems a little selfish on my part. HOWEVER, I am so turned on just by reading your e-mails, hearing about others who have experienced something deeper and more than I have, and I have to tell you, my mind is definitely straying.

He is a very tender and loving guy, and that used to be great, but I REALLY want him to take charge in the bedroom and lead me like you have talked about. Once he did get just a little rough and it really turned me on, as a matter of fact I know I came during doggie style when he bit me on the back and pulled my hair. He did not hurt me, just engaged other parts of my body.

He has a hard time with this because of his background I guess, but I am really frustrated. I have asked him point blank to get the materials to make our love more exciting but he is putting it off. DAMN!!! I wish I could get him to wake up and wake up the monster lurking just under the surface in me!! Any ideas what I can say to him to get him to wake up??

By the way, we have a religious background, which really is a problem for some people, probably those very skeptical readers who have bashed you, but I have to tell you, I believe those primal instincts are God given for a man and woman to desire each other in a loving relationship.

I just really wanted to write and say thanks for being you. Someone needed to figure these wonderful mysteries out and share them.

By the way, the way that you respond to the negative e-mails proves that you are a great guy and not a womanizer. I respect you and your work, thanks!

Thanks,

Very sexually frustrated

Here is an e-mail from Carol:

I was married for seventeen years. Things got a little stale.

I would try everything I could to "spice it up" but he kept saying he was "shy".

Eventually as life played out, I discovered that he was having his needs met elsewhere. We went into counseling for a year and I gave it my absolute all. I ended up getting better and he never did, so I decided to leave him. It was the hardest decision of my life... So here's where I am.

I want to be in a relationship, I'm not interested in casual sex... but I really, really want to have the experiences that you have described. To have a man take the lead, to be made love to in this way... I cannot even fathom it.

I am a 41 year old woman who is just aching to be made love to in the ways that you describe. How do I meet such a man?

I feel like a virgin all over again.

Here is an e-mail from Sarah:

I have found a guy that is just incredible! He is very sweet, funny and loving. He is not very experienced sexually and is a little uncomfortable with the subject. I know that he could be wild and crazy if I could just get him to come out of his shell. I desperately want to do that for him. I know that he would love it!

How do I get Mr. Polite to let down his guard a little and open up sexually. It would drive me crazy just to hear him even talk dirty! Help! I want to make all of his fantasies come true, but I first need to know what they are!

Thanks for any advice.

Here is an e-mail from Cassandra:

I wish my husband would read your material or any material. We have been together 16 years.

I am a successful business woman with a healthy sexual appetite. Maybe too healthy. I have to initiate sex. Talk about a blow to my ego.

What I really want is to be allowed to be submissive, to have someone who can let me receive pleasure instead of having to "give to get".

I am still in love with my husband but at this point I have to admit I am starting to look at other options. Life is too short not to experience pleasure.

Here is an e-mail from Carol:

I know your 'teachings' are geared toward men but I have read your "Manual" as well as your "Female Sexuality" book. I also subscribe to your e-newsletters.

My question is two-fold; I asked my husband to please read your Sexuality book. He has but has not yet put anything into 'practice'. When I read it, I actually thought "this is not him", "he will not be comfortable in this role" even though I desperately want him to. How do I help him get comfortable in the 'leader' role? How can I help him get started?

Your books/stories/teachings resonate so powerfully for me, I just want MY man to be this way. Help me help him please!

Here is an e-mail from Michelle:

Love your newsletters they are always very informative and certainly touch a spot with me. I do have an issue. I have just turned 44, physically attractive and do not seem to have a problem getting dates. What I am looking for is someone that can fulfill me sexually.

It seems like it should not be a problem however I am finding a lot of men do not want to explore this avenue. I try to bring it up in conversation on how I can please them more because of course I care about that as well. However they just seem to be happy with what we have and I want to grow in my sexuality. Any suggestions where I would find a like minded man?

Many thanks

Here is an e-mail from Denise:

As a woman, I find your description of the Masterful Lover very enticing. What I want to know is, where would I find a man like that?:)

Seriously.

Denise

Here is an e-mail from Macarena:

I now have a David-Shade-Deal-Breaker Clause. Once I'm ready to date again, not being a fan or practitioner of this material will be a deal breaker... and unfortunately, finding a natural would be virtually impossible since Casanova is long gone. But, thank God there's hope... thanks to David Shade!

Men are shown up by a lesbian. Here is an email from Candy:

David,

Being a woman (lesbian) and reading this profound information that you provided these "not so knowledgeable" men about women, I appreciate the fact that you had a passion for pleasing women and even defining the terms on how to please a woman and what makes her feel like the slut she desires to be in the bedroom.

You have given an all new meaning to what an orgasm feels like to women and the treasure of that blissful union of being incredible erotic.

To be brutally honest with you David, I have walked both sides of the fence. When I was younger and unconscious I slept with several men and they could not sexually satisfy me.

The thing that turns me on about women is that they have passion, compassion and intimacy. Women crave this and these are some of the feelings that some men are unconscious to taping into. If whether it be male or female, one can tap into the sensuality of a woman. With passion one can go a very long way.

When will these egotistical, self-centered men get a clue of what it means to really step up to the plate and be that man with a clear conscious. Step outside the box all of you men and support your gender as being men.

This knowledge and information that you have provided for men is all so very true. My props to you David Shade.

Peace and harmony.

CHAPTER 13
DO WOMEN HAVE ALL THE POWER?

"Then suddenly I was hit with a revelation.
The way a woman's body is made, the way a man's body responds to it.
The fire burning in my loins, the intense desire to merge as one.
It all came together in one brilliant flash."
~Don Juan DeMarco

Men complain that a woman can walk into any bar and take a man home in five minutes. From that, men conclude that women have all the power.

If you are a man playing the game of who can score a member of the opposite sex in five minutes, you lose. Most women have you beat at that game very easily. Does that make you feel defeated right out of the gate? That is not a very empowering perspective on things. If you have that defeatist attitude, you have already lost.

If you were to observe reality (by taking a seat in any bar and watching what really happens), you will find that women typically go into a bar with their friends and make an evening of it. What does that tell you? Reality tells you that women don't play that game.

Why is that?

To understand this, look at it from a woman's perspective. An attractive woman would be offered free drinks. She would not have to put air in her tires. However, it is because men want her just for her looks. In other words, she would be objectified, and being objectified makes her less than a person.

What if an attractive woman did walk into any bar and take a man home in five minutes? She would not know him. The sex would probably suck. She risks getting pregnant. She knows that she would just be an object for the man to masturbate inside of, and then the guy would think of her as a slut (in the bad way).

So, if women typically go into a bar with their friends and make an evening of it, then what game are they playing? What do they want?

I have already discussed at length what a woman really wants. She wants to be with a man with whom she will be fulfilled. But the reality of the situation is that all too many women are unfulfilled. They do not feel powerful; they feel frustrated that they can't find what they really want. On top of that, so many women are frustrated that they do not have orgasms in sex.

Reality points to the fact that women have all the frustration.

Women do not believe they are powerful because they could get laid in five minutes. For them, there is no power in that. It is not even considered. It means nothing to her. Women do not believe they have any granted power to get what they want.

What she really wants is to be with a real man—a man who will make her do things she is too inhibited, but deep down inside really wants to do. She wants to be with a man who's going to bring out that ruthlessly expressive, animalistic, natural sexual creature in her, a man who she can totally surrender to and be swept away with.

Only with such a man can she have all that she needs. As a result, one could conclude that the men have all the power.

However, the healthy way to look at it is that it takes two to Tango. You are the masculine compliment to her femininity. She is the feminine compliment to your masculinity.

Do not think about "getting sex." Instead, think about obliging her need for "really good sex."

CHAPTER 14
HOW WOMEN CATEGORIZE MEN

"The secret is seduction through temptation - make your life congruent with her fantasies and let her seduce you."
~Mark Cunningham

Some men have said, "On the first night, we get most of our clothes off, and I start fingering her. She gets off, then says, 'I've already gotten what I wanted tonight,' and I end up getting nothing."

That kind of thing happens on occasion with young women, especially if it is on the first night that you met her.

As for more mature women, they are more self-assured, interested in the man's pleasure, and decisive. If she goes home with a guy, it's because she has already made the decision that she is going to fuck him. If he gets her off before intercourse, she is even happier about her decision to fuck him.

As for mature high self-esteem women, they are especially interested in the man being excited about being with her. (This is in contrast to women with low self-esteem, who are looking for validation.) Also, they usually wait for the second or third date to let things go to intimacy.

Some mature high self-esteem women will only go as far as third base the first night of intimacy as a test of two things: 1) if she can she trust him, and 2) to see if she is still in control. It is also a test to see if he respects her enough to wait until the next night to have intercourse.

On top of that, for the very discriminating, highly sexual women, it is also a test to see if he can give awesome foreplay. These are the really fun girls!

In these situations (which you will find yourself in if you choose wisely), she is looking for a lover who is very good. If you have chosen well, awesome foreplay is in order. It will probably happen on the second or third date. Intercourse will happen on the next date.

Which brings us to the classic question: What are the long-term ramifications of closing her the first night you meet her versus the second or third date?

Let's look at two highly contrasting e-mails from two men:

Hi David,

I ordered your manual today and I think I have an important question. Your answer might be very interesting for at least some of your customers:

How am I able to avoid the girl/woman who wants a relationship?

I've been into a serious relationship for more than 12 years (I'm 32). Me and my girl broke up only a few months ago, so all I want to have at the moment is a good time. I'm successful with women, even the very beautiful ones - I think too successful...

I don't know what I'm doing "wrong". They all want a relationship with me. (I know this sounds weird since a lot of men out there would give their right arm for having my "problem".) I have not met a girl within the last few months (and there've been a lot) who would be satisfied by just having fun with me.

Since I'm not the type of guy who lies to girls to get what he wants there are only two things that happen again and again:

1. I know/feel what she really wants and I withdraw because that's something I don't want.

2. We do have "a good time" (at that point she already knows I do not want a relationship). The girl falls in love and there's drama afterwards. (I guess I better not read your book — it might be even worse afterwards. Lol.)

    What can I do to avoid the girl/woman who wants more and still feel really satisfied? What can I do to prevent her from feeling like a slut by having a one-night stand or an affair with me?

    Thanks for your help.

    Mike

Mike, it is okay to not want a relationship, and you certainly are not in any condition to have one, since you recently ended a very long relationship. I hope you spent some time alone to get to know yourself again.

It is perfectly normal for a woman to want to have a relationship, and, certainly, her being in a relationship reduces her "slut" concern.

Nevertheless, there are plenty of women who don't want a relationship, but still want to have intimacy. They just want someone they are attracted to, that they feel comfortable with, and that they feel safe with. They don't need all the other stuff that comes with being in a "relationship."

This can be found with women who just got out of a long relationship themselves (and had taken sufficient time off to get to know themselves again).

Also, this can be found among women who are very busy with some educational or career goal. They want to have fun, but don't want to be dedicated to a relationship. A lot of these women are high self-esteem women.

High self-esteem women who WANT a relationship are not going to waste their time with you. High self-esteem women who do NOT want a relationship would be happy to agree to your terms.

However, you're not attracting them (or you are, but you don't recognize it or you give up too quickly).

That leaves low self-esteem women. Low self-esteem women would put themselves through the agony of trying to convert you so they can get validation. They don't think enough of themselves to avoid the drama.

Speaking of drama, you mentioned that term. It is a term typically used to describe the lives of women who have low self-esteem.

If you are getting drama, you need to improve your screening skills.

Another possibility is that you are "doing" things that are in contradiction to what you "say." Women with either high or low self-esteem are going to go by your actions more than your words. You may "say" that you don't want a relationship, but the things that you "do" are viewed by the women as being congruent with starting a relationship.

Finally, yes, you absolutely must read my book when you receive it. It will give you a much clearer picture of all this.

Here is an e-mail from Gary:

```
Hello there, Mr. Shade,

    I've been reading a lot of your material.
It's certainly helped me to have more
fantastic one-night stands (many, many of
these!). I still feel that I'm having
trouble turning these into relationships
though. I'm not sure if I'm going too far on
the first night (i.e. offering everything,
becoming a girl's dirty, domineering fantasy
straight away) or, perhaps more likely,
```

mishandling things over the following days (I normally text the girl within 48 hours).

I was just wondering what you thought about:

1) How far to go on the first night, and perhaps in more detail.

2) How to handle the follow-up if I am interested in repeating the night, with the possible view to turning it into a relationship (gradually of course).

Btw - it's not that I go explicitly puppy love on the girl straight away, far from it, but after a great night I can't help feeling enthused and texting sooner and perhaps more excitedly than I would otherwise, fearing that it will go dead if I don't.

Well, many thanks for your time. They should teach your stuff to guys in schools. Really, that would save us all so much time and would probably get us evolving faster....

Best regards,

Gary

Gary, most men eventually find a really exciting woman that they are very interested in and wish they could see more. Unfortunately, that outcome seems to elude some of those men.

In order to feel those really deep emotions that are really exciting, and in order to do the "really advanced" stuff, it requires an interaction that goes far beyond one night. So, let's talk about how to make that happen.

First, let me say two things: do not be in love with the idea of being in love. A lot of men have that problem.

What they end up doing is choosing a person who is not right for them, and certainly the relationship would be for all the wrong reasons, i.e. out of need. Being in a relationship is a reward. It is not a goal to seek. It is something that two people create together based on what they develop together as a result of who they are. To seek a relationship is to take away from the genuineness of it.

Second, do not be afraid to be alone. It is better to be alone than with the wrong person. Believe enough in yourself to know that you will find what it is you require in a person. Have the self-respect enough to not stay with a person who is wrong for you, and have the self-esteem enough to be attractive to the really worthy women.

Now, to answer your two specific questions:

1) How far to go on the first night?

> If you want to see her again, do NOT go all the way on the first night!

2) How to handle the follow-up?

> If you violate 1), then no matter what you do for follow up, you won't see her again, usually.

> From your e-mail, it sounds like you regularly violate number 1.

For some women, if she has a one-night stand, no matter how good he was in bed, she feels cheap. She will not see him again because she knows that he will never respect her as much as she'd like.

For other women, whether she specifically set out for a one-night fling or not, if she meets a man she finds attractive, and he pushes hard for the first night close, she just may take him up on it for the fling of it, but that is all she sees him as. She has made the conscious decision to reduce the respect she has for him. He is not good enough for a relationship; he is only good enough for a one-night stand.

Now, there are exceptions. I know a young couple who consummated their relationship the first night they met. They have been together for over a year and are very happy, but it is the exception.

Women tend to put men into categories – one-night stand, relationship material, fuck buddy, just a friend, loser. There is no overlap. If she wants an anonymous one-night stand, she never sees him again. If she wants him for a relationship, she works on earning his respect.

Sometimes, a woman can be moved from one category to another. There are countless examples of successful relationships that started as friends and moved to lovers (but deeper inspection shows that most of those probably had some sexual tension all along).

It depends on the categories...

One-night stands rarely convert to relationships. Since a one-night stand is usually only about sex, she believes that the man views her only as a sex object, and she does not believe he could ever view her seriously. She believes that he could never respect her as a person.

Similarly, a fuck buddy arrangement rarely converts to a relationship. Usually, the fuck buddy arrangement eventually ends when one of the people moves to a relationship with someone else.

Interestingly, there have been a number of situations where I have converted a relationship to a fuck buddy, but I was unable to do it DURING the relationship, because that would violate the premise of a relationship. What I did was to tell her "let's just be friends." Then later, as friends and after some time had passed, we would reminisce about the great sex, and I would propose the fuck buddy idea. Since we were no longer in a relationship and she already knew me to be an exciting lover, it was okay. In fact, if she didn't really want to look for a new relationship but just wanted to have hot sex, it was a good thing.

There are rules for each category, and the woman follows the rules.

Women Follow the Rules of Each Category,
and Only When it Does Not Violate
Other Current Standing Rules

Don't be surprised if they DO stick to the rules! If you set yourself up as a once in a lifetime adventure, "It's Now or Never Baby," then don't be surprised if they take you up on it and then never come back! Even if the sex was good.

Why do women categorize some men into only one-night stands and others into only relationships? What makes her decide?

I thought it might be based on what she is looking for at the time. If she just wants a one-night stand, that's what she's going to look for. If she wants a relationship, that's what she's going to look for. However, I began to find contradictions to that. Many women have told me that they are looking for a relationship, but I end up closing them that night and never seeing them again. On other occasions, women have appeared to be moving things along very quickly but then won't let their panties be taken off, and then the next day talk about introducing me to the family.

Often, it appears that women don't know what they want, but I think most of them do. Ultimately, most of them would like to be in an exciting relationship with a very exciting person that they are completely fulfilled with and have everything they could have ever dreamed of. Sounds reasonable, but how often does that happen? What really is "ideal?" They have some learning to do. They need to have experiences.

They may meet an exciting man who does not meet all of their "relationship" criteria, but who would be fun to fuck, so they have a one-night stand.

Sometimes, they get into a relationship with a dependable person who might not be as exciting, but they want the companionship and regular sex.

Sometimes, they get drunk at the bar and meet an ideal relationship-material guy, but their inhibitions get displaced by their horniness, and they go for immediate gratification.

Basically, they fill the time. They learn on their journey.

Then, there are those women who want what they can't have – they're called mistresses – and then there are those women who truly don't know what the hell they want – they're called flakes.

Sometimes women take what works for them at the moment

Among my friends, I noticed that they were attracting certain kinds of women. Some of my buddies were always, and only, getting one-night stands, and others went from one long-term, committed relationship to another. Could it be that women SAW them as being in certain categories and went with that?

In those times that I drove hard for a first night close, I noticed that it would most often end up that way, and not in a relationship. On those times that I took my time, if anything, it ended up in a relationship.

Be careful what you wish for because...

Women go with the frame you present them

It all has to do with setting the proper frame. Decide what it is you want and present that frame. Act in a way that is congruent with what you seek. If you want a one-night stand, set that frame. If you want a relationship, set that frame.

Some might suggest that you first find out what the woman wants, and then meld to that, but often they give the wrong information, anyway. They may say they want a relationship, but only say that so they don't look like a slut when they fuck you that night. Some may move things along very quickly, but only to get into a position to sink their long-term relationship teeth in you. Most often, though, the woman is waiting for you to tell her what you want, so she can decide if she wants to play by those rules.

The best thing to do is to define the rules and then let her decide. Yeah, you may miss one or two on the way who may happen to be looking for something specifically different, but being indecisive is placating and results in far more lost opportunities.

Of course, there are exceptions to everything, and, of course, the rules change somewhat as women get older and more mature and more secure in themselves.

CHAPTER 15
THE SECRET TO GIVING WOMEN WILD SCREAMING ORGASMS

*"She was astonished to find herself receptive to so much pleasure, for I
showed her many things she had considered fictions.
I did things to her that she did not feel she could ask me to do,
and I taught her that the slightest constraint spoils
the greatest pleasures."*
~Giacomo Casanova

Females have the biological imperative to reproduce. Natural selection has weeded out the ones who are not driven to have sex. Women have the chemistry to be sexual, in fact, horny.

The female orgasm serves two purposes. First, since it feels so good, she will want to do it often. Secondly, it serves to create muscle contractions that pull the sperm into the uterus.

Men have the biological imperative to reproduce. We are all very familiar with that. Men are also subconsciously driven to please women because it gives our sperm a better chance of making it to the egg. So, it is completely understandable that we want our woman to have an orgasm.

Female sexuality is a mental thing though, and the female orgasm is very much a subconscious thing. She cannot consciously will it to happen. Similarly, if her subconscious objects to having an orgasm, for whatever reason, it will not happen.

Therefore, you must appeal to her mental sexuality.

While women have the chemistry to be sexual, it has absolutely no affect if the mental is not there.

Take for example the many recently divorced women that I had spoken with. In almost every case, she had become bored with her husband. Basically, she lost respect for him.

The interesting thing is, she was no longer excited about sex. She may have even stopped having orgasms. She no longer could get aroused. She could not even get excited through fantasies. She didn't even masturbate anymore.

She would actually become convinced that there was something wrong with her.

Then, she would get divorced. After some time, she would start dating again and go through a string of dorks and jerks.

Then... she would meet an exciting man, a man who stimulates her mind, who leads her, who brings out in her that sexual creature that yearns to live. She becomes highly sexual and can't get it enough.

This illustrates how female sexuality is all mental. It completely overrides anything chemical.

MENTAL ORGASM

The most important lesson I learned from my phone sex period is that female sexuality is all mental. That is where the real power is.

I had become very good at giving women amazing phone sex using very descriptive narrative of what I would do if I were there. So, I thought I'd push things even further.

I'd see if my voice alone could give her an orgasm. No stimulation whatsoever.

I would ask the woman which hand she was holding the phone with. Then, I'd tell her to place her other hand behind her head and keep it there.

Then, I would go into my usual narrative, but I would go into much more detail, excruciating detail.

I would start slowly and softly and sensually. That would go for about five minutes. Then, I'd build it up a bit louder and a bit faster and more sexual for about four minutes. Then, I'd go with very fast and loud vulgar description for about another two minutes.

Then, they would have an orgasm!

An orgasm created by only the brain—no physical stimulation whatsoever.

Of course, they would be flabbergasted. They loved it.

This happened with many other women. It was always very consistent.

Since female sexuality is such a mental thing, I wanted the most powerful tool possible to leverage that, so I learned hypnosis.

Then, things REALLY started to take off...

Since I could give a woman a mental orgasm, I wondered if I could give a woman an INSTANT orgasm, by simply telling her to come.

INSTANT ORGASM

After I made her come mentally, I'd let her rest for a while, and then I'd hypnotize her. This worked both over the phone and in person.

While she was under hypnosis, I'd simply tell her that when I say the words "come now" she will instantly have an orgasm.

Then I'd say, "Come NOW!" She would INSTANTLY have an orgasm!

After her orgasm subsided, I'd let her rest for only a few seconds, and then I'd say, "Come NOW!"

She would instantly have ANOTHER orgasm!

I would repeat the exercise enough times to make it permanently reliable.

Then, even after hypnosis or on another day, I'd fire it off as many times as I wanted! Fun stuff.

This has also been very consistent across women.

EXTENDED ORGASM

The female orgasm has always fascinated me. It usually lasts for about 20 seconds. I wondered if I could extend it out further.

I learned from my phone sex period that I could extend a woman's orgasm out another 20 or 30 seconds by telling her right when she starts to come that I am about to come. Women love it when their man comes, and they want to come at the same time.

When she started coming I'd enthusiastically tell her that I am going to come. I'd tell her to keep coming because I am about to come.

After her orgasm had gone for about 20 seconds, I'd grunt deeply like I was coming and tell her to keep coming. I'd make it very vocal and lasting for about 20 seconds. By doing this, I could get her orgasm to extend out to a minute.

I wondered if I could extend it out for as much as five minutes!

I just wouldn't be able to do it by continually telling her that I was about to come.

Since I had mastered the female orgasm through mental, I figured I could leverage that.

I'd cause a mental orgasm. Then, with hypnosis, I'd create an instant orgasm. Then another.

I would work her up to such an orgasmic frenzy that she was totally lost in it all.

Then, I'd create one more instant orgasm and I would simply TELL her that she was coming so hard that she can't stop coming until I tell her to.

She would keep coming!

I would continue the intense vulgar narrative to keep her going.

This went on way beyond five minutes! It went on indefinitely!

I would get women to come for an entire HOUR!

Knowing what I learned from hypnosis, I decided to try doing it without any hypnosis. I got it to work!

I didn't have to hypnotize a woman, after all, and it was very consistent across women. They could all do it.

This further illustrates the fact that female sexuality is 100% mental.

Orgasms are the convincer. When she is having wild, screaming orgasms beyond anything she has ever experienced or even imagined, she is convinced that her man has a powerful sexual power over her.

Orgasms are addictive. A woman will become so addicted to the extended incredible feelings and the neurotransmitters that she will HAVE to keep getting them! It causes her to become VERY bonded to her man.

SECTION 2

BE THE MASTERFUL LOVER WOMEN CRAVE

CHAPTER 16
HOW TO BE A MASTERFUL LOVER

"Women really love men who love women.
Women respect men who respect women.
And women go absolutely crazed-weasel wild over a man who obviously
knows how to please and satisfy a woman."
~Mark Cunningham

You love women. You are fascinated by women. You adore everything that defines a woman as woman. You derive no greater pleasure than giving a woman the most powerful, long-lasting pleasure of her entire life.

A woman is most fulfilled when she is wildly crazy about her man, when she feels beautiful and feminine and sexy, when she feels naughty, when she is aroused beyond description, when she can't get enough.

You appreciate the massive pent-up sexual potential in a woman, and you bring that out in her until she surrenders herself completely to you, allowing herself to become totally naked to you in every way.

A woman's pleasure is very cerebral. Her mind is the most important factor. You drive her wild with desire.

You understand that women are highly sexual creatures that crave intimacy, and you are comfortable with her sexuality. Women are far more sexual than men. Women have elaborate intricate fantasies beyond anything men can imagine. For women, it is largely mental and emotional, and about being swept away.

Being a Masterful Lover is about being personally and sensually powerful.

Being personally powerful is about empowering beliefs, self-reliance, a sense of deservedness, and Being The Man.

Being sensually powerful is about enabling her to enjoy everything that comes with being a woman, by expanding her envelope of sexual experiences, and bringing out in her that ruthlessly expressive, natural woman.

Everything you need to completely fulfill a woman is already within her. You bring it all out in her because you command respect, you earn trust, and you lead her.

Too many men see women as an obstacle to get around so they can get to the sex. Such men are just masturbating inside an object.

What you are seeking so relentlessly is nothing that comes from outside of you; it's something you already have.

The key to having what you want is not getting what you want, but being the person for whom getting what you want is a mere byproduct of the reality you create simply by the way you live life.

It builds a foundation of belief that is very real and a relationship with reality that is very empowering.

It is about two people celebrating being human beings. She is the feminine complement to your masculinity. You are the masculine complement to her femininity.

She knows that you can make her think powerful thoughts and feel powerful emotions. She becomes ultra-responsive to you.

There is nothing more natural than a man and a woman being together.

Stop thinking about getting sex from women. Think about giving women really good sex. Women are highly sexual creatures, and you're the man who's going to oblige her needs!

You are the man who's going to leverage her emotional soul to connect with her, her romantic heart to entice her, her innate sensuality to excite her, and her downright horniness to satiate her, and then do it again and again, until she is delirious with pleasure, ecstatic about being a woman, totally loving life, and wildly crazy about you!

Does Size Matter?

*"If you think you can or you think you can't,
either way you're right."*
~Henry Ford

There is the classic belief that a large penis is the key to satisfying a woman.

When those recently divorced women from my phone sex era told me their husbands were such boring lovers, I asked them, "Did he have a small penis?" They replied, "Well, actually, no." When they told me of the exciting lover that they had an affair with, I asked them, "Did he have a big penis?" They replied, "Well, actually, no."

That is when I first started to question the contribution of penis size.

When the internet started to become popular, I met women online. I met a number of married women who were looking to have an affair because they were tired of getting skewered by their husband's big cock. They found their times with me to be "refreshing," as well as multi-orgasmic.

Even years later, I have ex-girlfriends coming back for more, while telling me about their current lovers with large dicks, saying, "But he doesn't make me feel what I used to feel."

Here is an e-mail that I received from a female reader of my newsletter, which is typical of many e-mails that I have received:

    I had sex with a man that had a medium size
    penis and I used to cum like crazy. Now I
    have met this other guy that is well endowed
    with a very nice size penis, but it is
    really hard for me to cum. Can you help me
    figure this out?

Here are some actual e-mails that I have received from men (who had not yet purchased any of my Masterful Lover products):

I have been either blessed or burdened
with a big penis. The woman I am with now
has lots of trouble taking in the whole
thing.

She said it feels like it's bottoming out
most of the time, to a very tender area
inside, leaving her with a very
uncomfortable feeling.

If in the missionary position, if I slide
in slowly, she's ok.

I can't go hog wild because it hurts her,
but if I don't go hog wild then I find it
hard to maintain an erection.

She has never had a vaginal orgasm. She
has only had orgasms through clitoral
stimulation.

I've been working with her trying to get
her to orgasm in the "G-spot" area, with no
success yet.

Do you have any suggestions or positions
that would make sex more enjoyable for her
and me?

In reply to your e-mail, I would say to you: She is not having orgasms in intercourse, so what's in it for her? The same old routine every time and she never comes. It gets boring, and the regular impaling against her tender cervix becomes downright irritating. It gets really old.

To give her her first vaginal orgasm, use your three and a half inch long middle finger on her deep spot, which isn't that "deep" actually. It's just "deeper" than the G spot. Once you do that, she'll be much more receptive to intercourse, though you're still going to have to choke up on your bat.

Here's another e-mail (complete with the misspellings):

> my girl has never had an orgasim. i have had
> sex with her four miserable times doing what
> i thought was "good" but failing miserably.
> How do i change the current from what was
> done to what should be done, causing her to
> have multiple orgasims and having her trust
> me despite my last performance? i have a big
> cock but, this is really humbeling to write
> you about my shortcommings, but not only do
> i need to change precendence verbally but
> more imporantly, physically.... going to buy
> your stuff bro, need help!!

You can tell a lot about a person based on whether they use an upper-case 'I' or a lower-case 'i' to refer to themselves.

Here's another e-mail:

> I recently got with a 23 year old female who
> told me that she has never gotten an orgasm
> from any guy whose penis size is under 10
> inches. I told her that I was an 8 and one
> night when we were having sex she said that
> she wasn't feeling any orgasms any time
> soon, so we stopped. I felt weird and tried
> finding new ways to give her an orgasm. What
> can I do to make her have a mind-blowing
> orgasm that will make her forget all about a
> man's size?

In reply to your e-mail, I would say to you: You may have always thought that you were big, but she's got you thinking that you're too small. She's good, and you're being a wimp.

She said that she has never had an orgasm from any guy under 10 inches. You took her challenge even though you didn't measure up. That puts you in the wimp position. You should have simply said, "Sorry, Honey, can't help you. I'm only an 8."

Possibly, is the order of things said in your story a little different? I can imagine a man trying to impress a woman by saying, "I have an 8 inch cock," and then the woman cutting him down to size by replying with, "I've never gotten an orgasm from any guy who's under 10 inches." She doesn't take you seriously anymore, and thus she is not going to respond to you in bed.

Frankly, I'm surprised she went to bed with you. She was probably curious to see what it was like to be with an 8 inch cock. Evidently disappointing.

Here's an e-mail from one of my clients:

> David, I am having the most incredible sex, as often as I want, and of course, I am giving her the best sex of her life and she can't get enough. Do you want to know the one thing she always asks me? She'll look at me after I've just taken her, or given her an orgasm over the phone, or told her that I am going to fuck her in her office, or anytime I am direct and tell her what I'm going to do? She looks at me expectantly and asks, "You're never going to change, right? This isn't some sort of trick? You'll always be this way, right?"
>
> She had two orgasms the other night before I even got in her all the way. I just stuck the head in and let it sit there and she had two - just from the head.
>
> This is, of course, a hot girl that is used to having men pursue her and wine and dine her, take her on private airplanes to movie premiers, etc, etc, etc.
>
> David, life is good. Life is oh, so fucking incredibly good.
>
> Thanks for showing us the way.
>
> Robert

For men's perspectives, the way you answer the size question is a matter of beliefs. I tell men, "If you think size matters, it matters. If you don't think size matters, it doesn't matter." Basically, do you want to have empowering beliefs or not? It is empowering beliefs that are going to enable you to give women orgasms.

Here is one man with very bad beliefs:

```
Hi David, my penis is only 5 1/4 inches
long. I'm 50 and I have never had sex. This
situation drove me crazy for 35 years. I was
depressed and down and used drugs until I
was 45. I don't know who I have to see for
help, who I can ask for advice? Now I'm
totally mentally OK, out of any drug or
alcohol, but still afraid to even talk to a
woman! Thanks for any advice.
```

What a waste! There are many women who are happily married and consistently having vaginal orgasms in intercourse with their 5 and 1/4 inch long husbands. Too bad that man can't get all those years back.

Now, for the perspective of women. The women who remark that they prefer a man who is largely endowed and are disappointed to find when a man is less than largely endowed are women who have never had a vaginal orgasm. As for the women who consistently have vaginal orgasms in intercourse, they do not believe size matters. They have vaginas that are awakened and responsive. They could have a vaginal orgasm with just a finger.

Interestingly, most of the complaints made by women that have to do with size are due to the pain of having their cervix hit when thoughtlessly impaled by their endowed husbands.

And regarding fingers, if a man's middle finger can give a woman the very first vaginal orgasm of her life with the deep spot, then how could size possibly matter? The fact of the matter is that size has no correlation to women having or not having vaginal orgasms.

The ultimate answer to the size question is that you are going to believe what you are going to believe. If you are not giving women vaginal orgasms in intercourse, you are going to think that you are not big enough, no matter how big you are.

Does Experience Matter?

Being a Masterful Lover has nothing to do with experience. It is all about knowledge and beliefs. Even a virgin can do it. Here is an email from John in Australia:

Hey David,

I emailed you a while back as a narcissistic virgin. When I think back, it was amazing the amount of excuses I used to make for myself to justify why I hadn't had sex with women. What amazes me most is the amount of importance and emphasis most of us seem to place on 'losing your virginity' when it is just all crap.

After reading your "Give Women Wild Screaming Orgasms" book it really hit home that to be a masterful lover, it really isn't about how many notches on your belt you have, it really is about knowledge and beliefs.

After I received your book I must have read it 5 or 6 times in the same night. I was fucking dumbfounded. After deciding what I expect from myself and what I expect from the women I wish to date I bought your CD's on dirty talk and setting the foundations for a wild sexual relationship.

A little while later I went out with a girl when I finally took the lead, and I took her home.

After we were kissing for a while I began to escalate, and as I started to take off her clothes I began to tell her that every time I touched and kissed her skin she became more aroused.

When she was fully naked I threw her on the bed and fingered her in her deep spot. When I started to go faster I asked if she wanted to come. I asked how badly does she want to come for me. I asked her if she wants me to make her come and she started shouting how badly she wants to come for me.

Dave it was like I was reading your book while I was fingering her. I couldn't believe it. What happened next completely shattered my reality. When I told her to come now, come hard for me baby, her whole body started to shake while she orgasmed!

Once she finished she regained consciousness she flipped on her hands and knees, looked at me and said "I want you to fuck the shit out of me!"

Man the rest is history, my entire beliefs have completely changed. Holy shit Dave I can't thank you enough. Sorry to have written a novel but I had to share my experience. You have seriously changed my life dramatically. I know the women I've dated have appreciated it too.

Thanks again David, you are an absolute champion.

- John

Here is an email from Tore in Norway:

Dear David Shade,

In your material you write that it's not the quantity that matters but the quality; this in reference to guys feeling inadequate because of virginity or lack of experience. And I am now writing to you with a testimonial on exactly that... Because I am 29 years old, had my first kiss 10 days ago, lost my virginity two days ago and yet managed to make her cum so hard that she wiped off a few tears after and couldn't stop smiling for many hours later and keeps calling me all the time to come over and spend the night.

It's so amazing that if I didn't experience it myself I would have called the story a lie.

Here's the story in detail, starting with me, the shy guy that felt inadequate because of the lack of experience. I met a girl at an online dating site, and we found it as a very good match when we went out for a quick drink. So we met again during the day a couple of times and then finally a proper date with a movie and a late dinner. We went back to her place, and up until now we'd been flirting and teasing, but hardly any touching at all and no kissing whatsoever. I was simply too nervous to escalate. I felt pretty silly being 29 years old not having the courage to kiss a girl that was into me. But the problem was that I'd never tried it before and was very worried about what people would think if they found out. So here I was on the verge to be exposed trying my best to let pride go so I could start getting some experience.

It was getting late and I was thinking about getting home, as I knew that I wouldn't find the courage to escalate things to a physical level this time either. I had never had the guts before, so I didn't have any reason to think otherwise. But getting transport home wasn't too easy, so when she offered for me to sleep over if I would act as a gentleman I accepted. And all kinds of things raced through my mind... did she mean for me to sleep in her bedroom or the sofa? I was filled with both tremendous fear going to the unknown and excitement as I deep down knew where this were heading.

The thing to remember here is the amount of fear that has been allowed to fill my head for years and years. I was almost twice the age most people have their sexual debut and was at a certain point in life on my way to accept that I was asexual and would spend the rest of my life masturbating alone.

The irony here is that I am actually pretty good-looking and have been told on several occasions that I am very attractive, so my problem was solely mental and related to self esteem. And the reason goes back to when I was 9 and was bullied because of my girlfriends. Boys that age are fearful of "girl-bugs" and pushed me around to kiss them. As a result I stayed away from girls, and the damage was never repaired as I stopped going to parties and social events and hence missed out on the social and sexual development that teenagers are supposed to go through.

A few years ago I realized this and starting working very hard on my self esteem and to be relaxed also in informal social settings such as parties. It has worked tremendously well, and me going out with this girl was something I saw as the end of the treatment and me fully healed.

So now that you know and understand the pressure and buildup in my head we can return to the bedroom where I was almost shaking with nervousness and almost hoping we would only sleep. I figured she would notice my nervousness, but hoped she would write it off as many are nervous the first time they sleep together.

We talked for a while and I was calming down when I thought that it was now or never and inched myself a little closer and leaned in to experience my very first kiss. We both enjoyed it, and despite some clumsiness it escalated into a lot of touching until the clothes were gone... and at this point I lost my erection. But I remembered from David's material that you must not lose your cool over loss of erection or premature ejaculation and that the girl will copy your reaction. So she will freak out only if you do... So I waved it off with a wink and said something like "ooops… we lost junior... probably just a bit of nervousness... he'll be back soon."

Then I asked if we could try something I had read about... the welcomed method, and she complied willingly. It's a technique described in detail in David's material so I figured I wouldn't be able to go wrong on that one. After that we both went to sleep as I figured that I would have my chance some other day and also confident that I had a good backup technique to satisfy her if junior would leave me again.

During the next day she teasingly asked me when was the first time I had sex, because she suspected that I was a virgin. But I just replied in the same teasing voice that the information was classified and only to be revealed at a later stage. She was puzzled and couldn't figure out if I was confirming or denying her suspicion, but left it at that. I didn't deny her the information out of fear of her reaction, but because I was afraid that it would cause me to feel inferior. And feeling inferior just increases insecurity which is something I definitively didn't need.

A few days I spent the night again, and lost junior due to nervousness again, but waved it off like last time. This time I tried the G-spot with great success and to my surprise I was ok with the temporary impotence because the nervousness was almost gone this time. What was most important to me was not to leave my woman unsatisfied, because I figured that a satisfied woman would make you confident as it removes a lot of the performance pressure.

And I was correct... The third night the erection was gone for a little while, but when I introduced the deep spot she was moaning and wriggling so hard in bed the erection came back and she begged me to f*** her, and she came so hard that she both laughed, cried and giggled after. She told me that she was deeply impressed because she had never ever before orgasmed the first time she slept with a guy.

And here I was... just lost my virginity and feeling SO PROUD that I could make a woman come like that. It completely blew my mind as I was expecting lousy sex and lots of practice before I could get anywhere near pleasing a woman properly. So yes David, it is the mindset and quality that matters, not the quantity!

My deepest thanks David.

Best Regards

Tore

Here is an email from Jon in California:

David,

I'm sure that I'll have questions for you at a later date. For now, I just want to commend your efforts.

The more women I meet, the more I realize that I'm lucky to have this attitude. I'm only 21 years old -- a senior in college. It seems that most men (and by most, I'm thinking 99%) around college age don't place enough importance on giving pleasure. Some don't even think about it. The predominant attitude is to *take* pleasure. Nearly every college woman I've talked about sex with has complained about that. I can't even get hard if I feel that my partner is not receptive to me; for others, however, they just don't seem to care. It's really sad. It's hard to believe that not every man on earth doesn't have the lover's mentality. It's too bad that they don't realize that to be an attentive lover is to inspire your partner to return the favor.

You, however, are enlightened. Your book is a springboard to bestowing true rapture upon women. As a virgin, I researched sex, learning as much as I could so that I would be competent during my first time. (And I was :-) Damn, that was nice!) But the Manual goes far beyond competency. You probably could mass-market it one day. (Not that everyone would deserve such knowledge.) I had such grand notions in my head, but I wasn't able to express them until I heard of you. Keep up the good work. Hopefully, I'll be able to meet you someday.

Jon

Here is an email from Sebastian in Sweden:

Hi David!

I am writing to you just to tell you how amazing your material is, and how you have really helped me improve my life in many ways.

When I started reading your books I was still a virgin. I was (and still am) 19 years old and as you can probably imagine sex is something that is a pretty common topic of discussion among me and my friends. Most of them lost their virginity when they were 15-16 years old, and they often talk about "fucking girls". Their problem is that the girls never stay.

The reason that I started taking interest in your material was that I really wanted to know how to please women, and how to make them really want me. I wanted them to feel that I was THE man to have in bed. And why? Because in my opinion, my sex would also be way much better if she was having the time of her life together with me.

I lost my virginity a couple of days ago. It went really well, because I was well prepared. I was seriously VERY surprised with the result. After the sex she told me that she had never been that wet before. I couldn't believe it, but she really convinced me. Did I mention that this girl was 30 years old? "I've had long term relationships with guys, but NEVER this wet." Yepp, I was happy when I walked home that morning.

You have really helped me take my self confidence to a completely new level. This is only the beginning, and I am loving it already. Thanks David, you're the man.

Sebastian

Here is an e-mail from Nathan in Vancouver:

I'd like to share a success story with you, one that shows how your writings have helped every part of my love life.

First off, before I'd come across your newsletter, I was a virgin (though I'd dated and been in relationships a bit) who had become obsessed with trying to learn pick-up techniques, etc., but coming from a place of insecurity. I thought that I needed to change myself into a bar star horn-dog who could and would pick up a dozen chicks in a night. Not surprisingly my success rate was low and my motivation was equally low. I knew that there was something wrong with my game.

One day, I came across you through an interview of you and was at first totally put off by this man who talked about women being dirty, sexual beings. However, after a few weeks I listened to the interview again and was blown away. I immediately signed up to your newsletter and, by chance, found a friend who was willing to lend me his copy of your Manual. In very little time, the concept of a Masterful Lover just clicked in my head, like it was the missing piece of the puzzle.

I had a girlfriend at the time I discovered your work but I had messed things up due to all the crazy ideas about seduction I'd had earlier so I cut her loose without any fear of loss. She appreciated my honesty and we're still friends.

Within 2 days of the breakup, I found and began to date an amazing woman (who I found thanks to my newfound confidence). I've been with her ever since and have kept blowing her away with dirty talk, fantasies, orgasms of all types, ultimately respecting every aspect of her femininity. As a result, she is always telling me how she feels so safe with me, how she wants to do crazy sexual

things with me that she never used to be
interested in, and how I make her feel like
a woman. All this from a girl that was a
virgin before she met me!

I truly feel like THE man now that
everything about my love life has improved
(the meetings, the emotional closeness, the
sex, and even the breakups!), and it's due
to you.

So thank you, and feel free to use this as
a success story in your e-mails or as a
testimonial for the power of your writings.

Here is an e-mail from Osagie:

I was a 28 years old virgin until 2 months
ago. My celibacy was born out of religious
reasons and some limiting beliefs, but
that's a story for another time.

After much introspection at the beginning
of this year, I decided to pursue a
relationship with a girl I was friendly
with. Although we often kissed and made out,
we never had intercourse. There were
actually subtle cues from her indicating she
wanted to take things further sexually, but
I was more than aware of my sexual ineptness
and performance anxiety. I knew if I wanted
to continue to keep her, I would need to arm
myself with the necessary skills regarding
making love to a woman.

Fortunately, I came across your material
while rummaging through information on the
Internet and immediately signed up for your
newsletters. The newsletters were thought-
provoking, prompting me to purchase your
"Give Women Wild Screaming Orgasms" program.

Without mincing words, the information
contained in your program was like dynamite

shattering all my limiting beliefs on sexual intercourse. One thing that really impressed me about the book is that you cut through all the fluff, presenting only the meat on the subject.

Knowledge, they say, is power! Armed with the facts from your book and a newly found confidence I finally had intercourse with my girlfriend. The experience was ethereal. Even Mr. Webster can't describe how beautiful the experience was. Like you taught in your book, I led in the bedroom and she followed. She practically browned out when I applied the Welcomed Method on her and applied the deep spot technique. In fact, at a point she was so overwhelmed, she started panting like she was in a trance. I had never seen anything like it. I must admit I was a little scared until she held onto me and said she had never experienced anything so pleasurable until now!

In retrospect, I have come to realize that being good in bed is not about experience or how many lays you have under your belt. Rather it's all about knowledge and skill.

I can't thank you enough.

Does Longevity Matter?

When men concentrate on not coming too soon, that is exactly what happens. Maybe they should instead concentrate on her pleasure?

Here is an email from Lehlohonolo in South Africa:

Hi David

First off I would like to express how fortunate I feel to have found your work at 20 years of age, I proudly own most of the products that you have created and well, you made the stuff you know how liberating it can be to discuss knowledge that is so powerful.

I've wanted to write to you a long time ago but have not had a chance to use much of your teachings as I discovered it while I was in the process of making some major changes in my life, and unfortunately certain priorities have over shadowed my sex life. Although lately with more free time I have available to me I have gotten a chance to test out and play around with the work from your products and WOW!!!

I just want you to understand where I'm coming from quickly, I was in general unhappy with my sexual performance as a whole, being young and inexperienced I'd get over excited and come too quickly and it was frustrating, I'd tell these girls all kinds of things about how I wanted them to explode and get them all hot but when the time came I couldn't walk the talk.

The final straw was while I was staying in England I some how seduced a stunning young blonde German girl. Even my friends couldn't believe it, she was a certified 10!

One night while out we where talking and while building rapport she told me about her past sexual experiences and how boring the guys where, and how they all just lasted barely enough for her to notice what happened. I took it as my cue and started talking about how I would be different, how I'm better and basically promised her the fuck of her life.

She was very excited and even decided we need to go be alone ;) Once we where alone in the room it was a sad, sad affair. A couple of minutes and boom there's me coming just like the rest of them. The look on her face was heart breaking it became very awkward and she left and I never saw her again. That's when I got fed up and started investing in your products.

That was a few months back; 3 days ago I gave a lovely young lady four orgasms using the deep spot method. I feel an enormous amount of pride right now feeling her pussy nearly break my fingers watching the look on her face, I was blown away. I'd never seen that before and I made a wonderful little discovery. I thought she'd be tired after coming but bloody hell NO!!! She just wanted more! I can't stop laughing thinking about the contrast in how males and females react after an orgasm, she was ready to go just like that, well after she caught her breath of course, haha.

I am working on getting my life together at this point in time, as a man I'm working on being someone I respect. I am working on my life and my beliefs to be the kind of man that the worthy ones can be attracted to.

If you think it would help I'd be more than happy for you to use my words as a testimonial, if it will help some one out there to take responsibility and commit to improving themselves.

Something you mention that I'm finding is helping me be better at this stuff is the realization that I was being selfish and concentrating solely on my pleasure, when I cum, where I cum, how is my orgasm. It's not about me, it's about her liberation, about letting that wonderfully sexual woman inside her come alive and express herself. This is something I'm trying to ingrain into my psyche and already things are beginning to change. Women I'm sexually involved with are

behaving differently, it's hard to describe,
its like their aura changes to one of being
sexually comfortable even the way they touch
me. Like I said it's hard to describe but
it's fascinating for me to see.

You can rest assured that I will continue
to explore and use your teachings. I have
been holding myself back to an extent and
have been ignoring the power of my voice.
Well no more, it's time to shatter some
realities, theirs and mine.

Your Student Lehlohonolo

With the German 10 girl, he put it in right away and blew it. But
then, with the lovely young lady 3 days ago, he took my advice
and he used his finger to first give her vaginal orgasms, and she
wanted even more.

You can simply stick it in and blow it, or you can concentrate
on her pleasure.

Here is an email from Adam in Montreal:

Hi David,

I'm writing a quick note to say thank you
for all the fantastic products you're
putting out.

After I bought the cheapest one I could
find (I'm on a student budget) I was so
impressed by not only the information, but
by honesty with which it is given, that I
bought every product you have available,
because I had no doubt as to their value for
my money.

My girlfriend of 3 years and I are both
VERY satisfied with the results... I'll
mention specifically the Sexy Dirty Talk,
because when I started using it my
girlfriend would look at me wide-eyed after

coming harder than she ever had, and say "What the hell just happened?? Oh my god you're amazing!"

An unexpected added benefit is that I no longer have any trouble controlling myself, if you know what I mean, as a result of what I've learned. Thanks so much, really, and all the best to you.

Adam

The Correct Motivation and Intent

Don't think about getting sex. Instead, think about giving her really good sex. There is certainly opportunity out there. That is the correct motivation.

The correct intent is to bring out the decadent, primal, carnal, insatiably hungry, ruthlessly expressive, natural sexual woman in her. That will drive all the rest.

Ultimately, all of us men want to feel like a man. We have various ways of experiencing that. Some of us look for it in sexual conquests. For some, it is conquests of power or money. For most men, however, I have found that he really feels like a man when his woman believes in him completely and does all those naughty taboo things with him.

Napoleon Hill wrote that "man's greatest motivating force is to please woman."

If a man is with a woman he can't please, he will go on to the next one, and women need to understand that it is very important to him to please her. If she doesn't give him that opportunity, he will go find a woman who will.

Genuinely LIKE Women

Many guys see women as the obstacle to get around to get to the sex. Wrong!

Many men are angry with women. They blame all women for the few women who dumped them or shunned them. Wrong! There is not a grand scheme among women against you. Quite the contrary. Women are actually hoping for men. Women honestly and truly want men to fulfill women. However, women usually cannot articulate how men can fulfill women.

Instead, believe in women. Have empathy and compassion for women. Be fascinated by women. Genuinely get to know and understand women. The more you do, the more fun it becomes.

Command Respect

In order for your woman to be responsive to you, she must take what you say seriously. In order for her to take what you say seriously, she must have respect for you.

Expect that you will be treated with respect. Treat others with respect. Associate only with those who treat you with respect. Treat yourself with respect. A woman can only have respect for you if you treat yourself with respect.

At the same time, respect the fact that she wants to get slutty!

Earn Her Trust

In order for her to surrender to you completely, she must trust you completely. You must earn her trust. You do this by demonstrating that you are trustworthy.

This is very simple. Do not violate her trust. Do what you say you are going to do. Do not do what you say you are not going to do. Rise to the occasion in all the little opportunities that make themselves available for you to demonstrate that you are trustworthy.

Be a Man

An ex-girlfriend once told me, "It is the man you are outside of the bedroom that allows me to be the woman I can be inside the bedroom." Everything must go correctly outside the bedroom if you want everything to go correctly inside the bedroom.

Stand tall, tell the truth, live a life of integrity, and live up to your responsibilities.

Many men are afraid to be a man. As you look back, you can probably find that most of your bad decisions and failures can be directly attributed to the fact that you were afraid to be a man. I know I can certainly say that.

Those men who get told by women "let's just be friends" are men who are afraid to be men. They are afraid to assert their masculinity for fear that they will risk the friendship they have with the woman. They think that if they voice their attraction for her, that she will dismiss them. In some cases, it may happen, but certainly not in most. Such men are left in a drought.

Passion and Absolute Conviction

All of the men who are successful at bringing out the natural sexual creature in their woman are men who are passionate about it.

You must do this with absolute conviction, absolute determination. There can be no crack in your armor, there can be no crack in your voice, or it won't be believable. Only when it is believable, is it going to work. You are leading, and she will only follow if she sees you as believable.

Have a Plan

When you bring your woman out on a date, know what you are going to do. Know what time it is going to happen. Know where you are going to take her for dinner. Know where you are going to take her dancing. Of course, you are flexible, too. If she suggests something else, you can do that.

In our modern world, women are busy during the week with their lives, such as working, getting an education, and so forth. Women want to be respected for their intellect and accomplishments, as they should. That's all good. On the other hand, on Saturday night, she doesn't want to have the responsibilities of the date. She wants to feel like a woman. She wants to enjoy the classic role of being a woman. She wants the man to be the man.

That sets the basis for everything. It is a context in which the man leads and the woman follows.

Calibration

The truly skillful lover simply knows when his woman is ready. You should know when she is ready to be kissed. You should know when she is ready to be entered.

There are many tests out there that tell you how to know if she is ready to be kissed. You can run them, but you need to get to the point where you simply know.

The problem with running tests is that you are not as believable. You no longer come across as being in the lead. You are not as much of a sexual threat if you are testing. Instead, you should be calibrating and leading.

You will if you get out of your own head. Pay attention to her. Enjoy the process. Enjoy watching the changes in her.

Be Patient

Too many men are in a big hurry to get to the sex. That is a huge mistake.

Do not push against last minute resistance. You will be like all the other guys who objectify women and do not respect her as a real person, and it will reek of desperation.

Instead, defer your own gratification for the big goal. The big goal is to bring out that ruthlessly expressive sexual creature in her. It's going to take a little time before she becomes "Daddy's very naughty horny little cum slut fuck bitch."

In fact, move things along just slightly slower than she'd like it. Make her wait. It builds that sexual tension, and it makes her think. When she is away from you, she is going to think about it a lot, because it is that time away from you that she becomes close to you.

That is early in the relationship. Later in the relationship, there will be times when you will initiate sex when she least expects it.

Be Dominant

Most women are sexually submissive creatures. They respond to a dominant man. Be comfortable in that role.

Here's a good example. If she is wearing a T-shirt or a sweatshirt, pull the shirt over her head, but keep it on her arms. This lightly restrains her arms. It's called "The Hockey shirt trick."

While laying down and making out with her, hold her hands above her head.

While standing and making out with her, hold one hand behind her head and the other behind the small of her back. Then move her backwards until your elbows smash into the wall. She will not be hurt; your elbows will take all of the blow.

It is all symbolism. Many of these light restraints she could easily get out of, but it's the symbolism that is powerful.

Everything is Sex

"Sex is hardly ever about sex."
~Shirley MacLaine

Sex is not an act; it is a disposition. Take on a whole new way of thinking.

First, let's define some terms here. Most people think of foreplay, followed by sex. But in actuality, foreplay is sex. That's why it's called "oral sex." When people use the term sex, they usually mean intercourse. Intercourse is only one of the many things included in sex.

Think in a new way. Anything that you and her do to each other while naked in the bedroom is sex.

Actually, you don't have to be naked, and you don't have to be in the bedroom. You could be masturbating her while you two are at the movies. So, really sex is anything that you and her do to stimulate each other's genitals.

Actually, you don't have to be stimulating her genitals. You could be sitting with her at a restaurant and simply command her to have an instant orgasm. That is sex.

So, sex is basically anything that sexually stimulates her.

There are many things that sexually stimulate her. You could be narrating a sexual fantasy to her. That stimulates her sexually. So, simply narrating a fantasy is sex.

You could be telling her how you are going to make mad passionate love to her when you get her home. That stimulates her sexually. So, simply mentally preparing her for sex is sex.

There are many ways that you mentally prepare her for sex. You mentally prepare her for sex when you tell her that she looks beautiful to you. So, by definition, that could be considered sex.

I could go on. But basically, everything is sex. Live your life as a sexual person.

Show Her How Much She Turns You On

This is the magic dust of instant turn-on for her.

Women want nothing more than to know that they are desired. In the bedroom, tell her how much she turns you on. Demonstrate to her how much she turns you on. Tell her that you think of her when you masturbate.

During intercourse, especially at the climax, be expressive. Women love to know that their man is excited about them.

Do all these things. It works like magic.

Select Women Wisely

In his famous book, *"Think And Grow Rich,"* Napoleon Hill wrote, "The most important decision you will ever make is selection of a wife." That is so very true.

Success begins with selecting wisely, pure and simple. Select a woman who has these three things true about her:

High Self-Esteem

Intelligence

Sexual

HIGH SELF-ESTEEM:

Everything you need to completely fulfill a woman is already within her, but a woman can only be as fulfilled as she believes she deserves to be. Select one that believes she deserves it.

People don't get what they want; people don't get what they need. People get what they honestly and truly believe that they deserve. If a woman does not believe that she deserves to be happy, she will sabotage any attempts at happiness.

A sense of deservedness is a component of self-esteem. Self-esteem is defined as having two parts:

1) Confidence in our ability to learn, make appropriate choices and decisions, and respond effectively to change.

2) The belief that success, achievement, fulfillment, and happiness are right and natural for us.

At a conscious level, people say, "Of course, I expect to be loved. Of course, I deserve to be loved. Why shouldn't I?" But the deeper, negative feelings are there, operating to sabotage efforts at achieving fulfillment. Being subconsciously manipulated by one's own self-destructive and self-sabotaging beliefs can lead to irrational behavior. In other words, it can manifest itself in ways that seem to make no sense at all.

Self-esteem is formed early in life during the developmental years. For a little girl, it is the relationship with her father that is critically important. That is where she learns to trust a man and have a healthy emotional relationship with men. A woman who grew up with a close, loving, healthy relationship with her father is what I call a "Daddy's Girl."

INTELLIGENCE:

Sexuality for women is entirely mental, so the more intelligent she is, the more the mental aspects of female sexuality can be leveraged.

SEXUAL:

If you find a woman who has high self-esteem and is intelligent, there is an extremely good chance that she is sexual. But some women are more sexual than others. How sexual do you want to be?

For more information, see: SelectWomenWisely.com

Here is an e-mail from Jason:

```
David,

    I have a very good thing going with this
woman who is drop dead gorgeous (a solid
10), intelligent, highly sexual, and has a
good imagination. But, and it is indeed a
big but, she has fairly low self-esteem.

    I have tried alot of different things but
she simply will not "let go" and surrender
to me. I find this very frustrating because
I give her very good sex and I treat her
very well. We have had alot of stupid fights
because she gets very insecure if another
woman looks at me.

    My biggest worry is that she will not
surrender completely to me. She has already
many times said, that I'm the best fuck of
her life (Thank YOU David, you might want to
take a bow!!) but I feel like she hasn't had
all she can have.

    I've massaged her clit, her deep spot both
back/front, given her dirty talk and so on.
I have given her the best of me. I don't
```

hold back. Sometimes we go on like this for 4-5 hours. But she never comes!

I know you are going to ask me what her relationship with her father was. He was a drunk and mentally abused her and left the mother.

What can I do? I really like this woman and she is beautiful.

Now here is an e-mail from Robert:

Holy shit!!

All this stuff is starting to come together. David you are so on the money with high self-esteem and good relationship with her father.

I was having my doubts but believed in the material. I kept reading, re-reading, using it on women that I was dating, noticing the results, not making it mean anything about me if something wasn't producing the expected results.

But then it happened. I've met a high self-esteem woman who had a good relationship with her father, who follows where I lead without constantly challenging me, misdirecting or numb to feeling.

It is Over-the-TOP!!!

A woman that puts the WILD and SCREAMING into orgasms!!

I'm now experiencing a woman that can go into spasms and convulsions when I stroke her body with my eyes. A woman that responds orgastically to the power of my voice. A woman that begs me for my cock. A woman that cries tears of joy for the feelings that she feels. A woman that wants to do anything for me out of deep gratitude for how I can make her feel.

To put it in context, before your material I was confident in sexually pleasing a woman. I've had experiences of multiple orgasms, hour-long orgasms, but the wild screaming orgasms had been elusive. Frankly it stretched my paradigm. My confidence has deepened and expanded and continues to grow with each new experience.

O MY GOD...

I LOVE BEING A MASTERFUL LOVER!!! Giving a woman WILD SCREAMING ORGASMS is SO FULFILLING!!

THANK YOU DAVID!!! YOU ARE AWESOME!!!

You created a frame of belief where all this is not only possible but predictable. I am so appreciative. Thank you.

If it wasn't for you, I would not have been prepared when the opportunity presented itself. I was able to recognize it and lead with confidence. As you say, "It's all mental". IT'S SO TRUE!!!

THANK YOU!!!

CHAPTER 17

HOW TO UNLEASH HER INNER ANIMAL

"No matter how hard the shell,
they all have a soft, chewy center."
~David Shade

Again, this information only pertains to mentally healthy women. In fact, it best fits women who are intelligent, have high self-esteem, and are highly sexual.

When I say "women this" and "women that," I mean MOST women. Certainly, there are exceptions to everything.

Also, this only applies to women who you intend to see on a continuing basis. It does not apply to one-night stands. The most important reason for this is that only women who take you seriously are going to respond to this.

Remember, when you lead a woman, you are responsible for her. You must be a responsible leader.

Further, all of this is absolutely in the context of enhancing a relationship that is based on trust and intimacy. It is all for the enhancement of the relationship.

Basically, this stuff only works on "the really worthy ones", as it should.

This is not about having power over women. This is about "being powerful" and about "empowering her".

Most importantly, you want to get your woman to a point of total abandonment.

Always know that women actually like sex. A lot. They like it often, and they like it good. If a woman does not want sex often, it is because it is not good. Follow this general rule:

The Better It Is, The More She Has to Have It

Men think that if they give a woman really good sex, she is then satiated and does not need it again for a while. Nothing could be further from the truth. The fact of the matter is that the better the sex is, the more she has to have it. It is the women who are getting great sex from their man who think constantly about sex with their man.

Once they do have it, they become addicted to it. Nothing else ever compares. You can ruin it for all the other guys.

If the woman has been with a truly exciting lover before, that's actually a good thing, because she has to have it again. She will always long for it. Once she meets you and she begins to recognize that you can make her feel all those things again, she will powerfully respond.

Unleash Her Sexual Potential

Men need to understand that there is a massive amount of untapped sexual potential in every woman. It is there in a woman. Everything you need to fulfill a woman is already within her. You simply need to tap into that. Only a man can do that for her. Thus, men have a tremendous amount of power—more than they know.

What women want is a personally powerful man who will lead her through all those experiences that bring out the natural woman in her. Women may not know this, and they certainly are unable to articulate it, but it is exactly what they respond to. Such a man, in turn, is an extremely rare thing to find. Such a man has a tremendous amount of power, because she has to have that and she reacts so very powerfully to it.

Basis of All Interaction Between a Man and a Woman

The underlying basis of all social interaction between a man and a woman who just met is sexual, plain and simple. It is not articulated; it happens subconsciously. It is what is on both people's minds.

You are the masculine complement to her femininity. She is the feminine complement to your masculinity. There is nothing more natural and normal than a man and a woman getting together.

Romance

Romance is the socially acceptable term for sexuality. In the context of romance, sexuality is acceptable.

There is a lot of symbolism in romance. Take advantage of those symbols. Learn how to fold an ordinary paper napkin into a paper rose.

In the context of romance, she can begin to feel all those things that women want to feel. It's just like the romance novel.

You don't have to be in love to have romance, and you don't have to be in a classic dating situation to have romance. Also, being romantic does not mean that you are in a classic dating situation.

Romance elicits all the wonderful dreams she had as a little girl, and that is the context in which sexuality can emerge.

Emotional Connection

Emotional connection is the lubricant to sexuality.

Women are emotional creatures, and they want to feel connected to their man.

Establish that emotional connection. Allow her to emote, but don't let it go so far that you end up being her emotional pincushion.

Do not try to fix her problems. Women loathe that. Instead, have empathy for her and support her. Women love that.

Show your vulnerability to her. Allow yourself to emote to her slightly, not in a needy way, but in a way to convey connection and to slightly reveal your vulnerabilities.

How can you be an emotionally connected person but still be the man and command respect? Being emotionally connected is a manly thing. It is not contradictory.

It is only a wimpy thing when it is with lack of sexual threat. It is only wimpy when the man is sexually harmless.

Mental Foreplay

"For men, sex is sex. For women, sex is everything else."
~unknown

Women complain that their man wants to go from zero to a hundred in six seconds.

Men think that just going to bed means his woman is going to want sex. He turns to her, but she rejects his advances. A pattern has been set. Going to bed means he is going to want sex. In that case, sex is assumed. She knows that sex is a given. She is only going to do it if she feels like it, but nothing has been done to make her feel like it. That is boring for her and frustrating for him. It continually reduces her interest in sex.

You must not wait until going to bed to start seducing your woman. Once in bed, it is too late. Instead, you must always be seducing her. Seduction goes on all the time. This is done with "mental foreplay."

This concept of "mental foreplay" is the convergence of three important truisms:

1) Women want foreplay

2) Sexuality for women is entirely mental

3) Everything between you and your woman is sex

A woman once said, "If a man can fuck my mind, he can have me." She is articulating the mental aspects of female sexuality as "mind fuck." Let us instead refer to it in a less derogatory way as "mental sex." This goes back to my concept that "everything is sex." Furthermore, foreplay is sex, thus, it follows that "mental foreplay" is "mental sex." Backing all the way up, we see that mental sex begins with seduction.

Seduction must go on all the time. You must at all times be seducing your woman in some manner. It may be subtle; it may be obvious. But it must always be taking place. Women absolutely love being seduced. They love the way it feels. They feel beautiful and sexy. They feel desired. They get to feel all the things that women love to feel, and it results in them wanting to celebrate that. Even in an ongoing relationship, a woman wants to be seduced by her man. Always keep an air of sensuality. When your woman thinks of you, she must think thoughts of being seduced.

You can even do this when the two of you are apart. A great way is to send her text messages. They may be innocent messages with sexual innuendos, or they may be blatantly sexual.

The "It Just Happened" Clause

Everything you do must be in the context that she can simply say, "It just happened."

Do not articulate what is going to happen. Instead, simply lead her.

What is going to happen should never be articulated, or else for her to comply is for her to articulate what is going to happen, and to do so would define her as easy, a slut, or being in the lead. That is not the woman's role.

Instead, simply move things along slowly, but surely, using body language. Let her get lost in the passion.

She should always be able to justify it later by simply saying, "It just happened." Monday morning she can go into work and tell her girlfriends all about it, and then say, "It just happened," and they'll all swoon, because they know exactly what she's talking about; two people got swept away in passion.

There will be times later in the relationship when you can, and should, articulate what is going to happen, for effect.

The Importance of Naughty

Naughty is the enabling context for taboos.

Everything taboo that you bring her through will be done in the context of naughty. She's doing it because it's naughty, and that will get her through all those taboo things that she would never do.

When she's with you, because you drive like a man, you are dominant; simply tell her that she is being naughty. In that context, nothing is taboo.

Also, be sure to tell her that it turns you on! That will be her justification.

Dirty Talk

I cannot tell you how very important and how powerful this is. Your most powerful tool in the bedroom is not your tool; it is your voice. It is by far the most powerful tool.

A lot of men have trouble doing that. They are concerned that she will take it wrong, be offended or insulted, or that it would make her a slut.

Women don't want to be a slut, but they love to be slutty. In the right context, with her man that she trusts and respects, in privacy, under his care and direction and watchful eye, she loves to be slutty.

Start things slowly. Build the sexual arousal. Then, begin introducing the dirty talk. Let the sexual arousal increase. Be sure to do it with absolute conviction. It must be believable.

As the sexual arousal increases, the context changes. Everything you say in heightened sexual arousal is taken in a completely different context. She will not take it wrong, because:

In The Context of Heightened Sexual Arousal,
Everything is Taken in a Completely Different Context

It is all mental stimulation. I explain this in detail, including an interview giving a woman's opinion, in my program, "Give Women Wild Screaming Orgasms."

Phone Sex

Phone sex is dirty talk on steroids. In phone sex, you can get very raunchy, and she can respond powerfully to you. You start off easy and then slowly ramp it up to be extremely explicit and crude and rude.

You can get away with things in phone sex that you have not yet been able to get away with in person. Someday, they may be possible.

In phone sex, you bring her through experiences mentally. Once she has experienced it in her imagination, once she has made it real in her mind, and it is associated with heightened sexual arousal, she can later experience it in person.

Because it is phone sex, it is just a fantasy, and so she can go along with it, but once she experiences it in her mind, it has become real for her subconscious, and thus, it can later become true.

For excerpts of actual phone sex recordings, see: GiveWomenHotPhoneSex.com

New Orgasms in New Ways

Orgasms are the convincer! Without wild, screaming orgasms, nothing will work.

Give her new orgasms in new ways.

If she's never had an orgasm, give her her first orgasm. If she's never had a vaginal orgasm, give her a vaginal orgasm. If she's never had an anal orgasm, give her an anal orgasm. If she's never had a nipple orgasm, give her a nipple orgasm. If she's never had an instant orgasm on command, give her an instant orgasm on command. If she's never had an extended orgasm, give her an extended orgasm.

Bring her through these new experiences. They are powerful convincers that increase her responsiveness to you.

And it's not enough that you just give her orgasms, it's that you have a lot to say about when, how hard, and how long she has an orgasm. Interestingly, that's actually the way she prefers it!

Do Men Actually Give Women Orgasms?

It has been said that men don't actually GIVE women orgasms. Instead, women HAVE orgasms. That's all fine and good, IF women are actually HAVING orgasms. I really don't care if it is GIVE or HAVE, the important thing is orgasms.

But what about the women who are NOT having orgasms? What then? She can't HAVE orgasms. In that case, you have no choice but to GIVE!

And what about women who have orgasms by themselves, but not with their man?

Here is an e-mail from Donna:

```
David,
    I met a man after being single for 6 years
no sex, no nothing. I would just masturbate.
I can get myself to have an orgasm. Now that
I have a partner after all this time he
can't get me to. He feels so bad.
    I really care for him, we are all over
each other. I am 34, no kids. What is wrong
with me? Help. I want to make hot love with
him and let him hit the spot.
    HELP ME PLEASE WHAT DO I DO??? I'm not
letting him go, I've never felt so cared and
loved like this... HELP...
```

Orgasms are a subconscious thing. Women cannot consciously will themselves to have an orgasm. If women could, they'd just do it themselves!

A lot of women fake orgasms just to get it over with. Many married women do this regularly. Her husband has been pumping away for 20 minutes, and she knows she is not going to have an orgasm, so she fakes it just so he will stop and she can finally go to sleep. If she could have willed herself to have an orgasm, she would have done it long before, and often. In fact, she would be inspired to have intercourse often!

Now, it could be argued that a woman could simply masturbate and give herself an orgasm. But the fact of the matter is that when she masturbates, she thinks about a man GIVING her orgasms!

You could set up a research grant study in some university medical laboratory with a white lab coat and a clip board and have women volunteer for an experiment. They can only be women who can have orgasms. The women would be instructed to masturbate to orgasm, but they would not be allowed to fantasize. They are only supposed to cause themselves physiologically to have an orgasm, not psychologically. This would be verified with an MRI brain scan. If they fantasize, an MRI alarm would go off. "BEEEP!" Some of the women would probably be able to do it. But some of them would cheat and set off the alarm. And none of them would be back; they'd much prefer to masturbate to a fantasy.

I'm not saying that it's a bad thing that women typically don't masturbate just for it to feel good. I'm all for women making themselves feel good, knowing her body, and celebrating her body just for the sake of it. It's healthy. It's all good.

But it is not reality that women masturbate without fantasy, and that is certainly understandable. It's much more fun to fantasize!

As I have said many times, sexuality for a woman is entirely mental. It is the excitement of it all.

When a woman is with her man, the thing that is exciting for her is that he GIVES her orgasms. That is what it's all about. For her, it is not about two people getting together to HAVE orgasms, it is all about two lovers GIVING each other orgasms.

Every Woman Can Have Vaginal Orgasms in Intercourse

"There is no such thing as a difficult dog,
only an inexperienced owner."
~Barbara Woodhouse

You heard me right. Every woman. Some will get there quicker than others. Some are already there.

Each will require a different route. It may be as simple as applying the deep spot; it may be as complicated as her working with a professional psychologist to deal with deservedness issues or child sexual abuse. But absolutely every single woman can have vaginal orgasms from only penile-vaginal intercourse.

It may be hard to believe by the 70% of women who don't have vaginal orgasms. They think they are not "one of the lucky ones." There is no such thing as some women being preordained to have vaginal orgasms and some not. All women have a vagina and a mind.

It may be hard to believe by the men who think they are not big enough or don't last long enough. However, those two concerns have already been debunked.

One thing that it will most certainly require is that you drive like a man. You must lead her there.

You absolutely, positively must get this working. If you don't make this work, you have nothing. If you orgasm but she doesn't, then, from her perspective, sex is all about you. What's in it for her? If you do that over and over for decades, don't be surprised if her interest in sex goes away.

Here is an e-mail from Linda:

```
David,

    I have been married for 16 years and with
the same man for 20 years. I am a 36 year
old woman who is clitoris dependent in order
to have an orgasm. These don't come very
often and lately has began to really
frustrate me. I want so desperately to
experience those mind shattering vaginal
orgasms that your clients talk about!

    I've experienced a couple beginnings of
vaginal orgasms but then it stops. What
little I've felt makes me want more. My sex
```

drive has reverted to that of a teenager now
:o)

I was surfing the web trying to find out
what I could about the female orgasm when I
ran across your site. I had almost reverted
to the thought that vaginal orgasms don't
happen. That women on dvd/tv were just
faking it.

You are right on so many things.
Especially about the fact of what we want.
We are just afraid to ask for it.

I ordered your book on giving women wild
screaming orgasms for my husband and myself.
I can't wait to get it!

I want to feel pleasure every time we have
sex. I want to experience vaginal orgasms on
a regular basis. I hope I'm not being
selfish but I want to orgasm every time
since he gets to.

Is it too bold for me to tell him that
there will be no more sex until he finishes
your course? Can your book help me as a
woman?

Linda

I sent this email to her...

Linda, you are clitoris dependent from decades of diligent
practice. Of course, those women on DVDs are faking it. It's all
for show. But I assure you, vaginal orgasms exist. ANY woman
can have them.

Yes, my program "Give Women Wild Screaming Orgasms" can
help you. Your man must read it cover to cover, and he must listen
to each and every CD. And then, in the bedroom, you must do
exactly as he says. Surrender to your husband, and trust the
material.

Look at it this way, if you could do it yourself, you'd have done it a long time ago. I however, and all of my top clients, have collectively given countless women their very first vaginal orgasm in intercourse. Your husband will do the same for you. Don't get in his way, or yours. Enjoy...

A few weeks later, I received this email from Linda:

David,

First of all, Thanks for your program!! However, now it is all I can think about!! I think I now know what it is like to be a man (in regards to thinking about it all the time)!!

When my husband began massaging my deep spot I started to feel it from my head all the way down to my toes. Before I could even tell him I was getting ready to come it happened and he knew it. It was wonderful!!

Just the other night I had my first vaginal orgasm while he was inside me. OMG! It was wonderful :) It just keeps getting better and better and I can't wait for the next time! I think about it quite often!! I can't get enough!

I'm an accountant and am having a terrible time focusing at work! For instance, today... my husband is out of town and I couldn't focus for the life of me so I ended up having to go home for lunch and take care of things myself :) He has definitely released the animal in me!

I feel as though I am more sexual than him now! Any suggestions on how to get my focus back? I definitely don't want to go back to how things were before!! This is soooooo much better ;) Thanks David!!

Linda

The "Yes" Ladder

Lawyers have a saying, "A lawyer never asks a question in court that he does not already know the answer to." I would add to that, "A true lover never asks a question in bed that he does not already know the answer to be 'Yes.'"

Get her sequentially saying yes.

"You love it when I do this." "Yes."

"It feels so good when I do this." "Yes."

"This makes you so excited, doesn't it?" "Yes."

"You want me to ____." "Yes."

This sets up a pattern for her following your lead.

Fantasies and Role-Play

Get to know her fantasies. Describe them back to her as you masturbate her.

Make up some fantasies. Lead her mentally through those fantasies as you masturbate her.

Introduce new fantasies using phone sex.

Use role-play to act out fantasies. Since it's just "make-believe," she can feel much more comfortable about playing the part.

Once she has played the part, it has become real for her in her mind, and she is much more apt to actually do it for real.

Expand Her Sexual Experiences

With you, she's going to do all those things she dreamed about experiencing, and even some she never dreamed about.

You are going to lead her through these experiences, such that you and she are going to experience these things together in real life.

You are always pushing the envelope just a little bit—little baby steps at a time.

All of these things that you bring her through continue to open her up and continue to release that massive sexual potential.

The Power of Possessive

It is a bad thing to be possessive of your woman from a relationship standpoint. It demonstrates fear and weakness.

However, in the context of heightened sexual arousal, it is a very powerful thing to be possessive of your woman.

"Who's naughty little slut are you?" "Yours, Daddy."

Piece of Property

For the really advanced level (brace yourself), treat her like a piece of property.

At a fetish party, my girlfriend at the time and I once saw a man pulling his beautiful wife around by a collar and leash. We befriended them. It turns out the woman was a bank senior vice president with an Ivy League degree. She just happened to be very sexually submissive. She was also madly in love with her husband.

Make her wear lingerie and heels around the house as you ignore her. After doing this for an appropriate amount of time, you then take her and use her to get off. Use with a thick application of dirty talk. Not for the faint at heart.

Of course, all of this is done in the context of equality in all other areas and in the context of absolute respect. In the context of absolute respect for her, she is secure in knowing that she is your special woman, you are ultimately doing this for her sexual fulfillment, and she can let go and totally surrender to the passion. In this context, she can assume the 'role' of being your piece of property, which is the ultimate expression of sexuality for a sexually submissive woman.

Total Surrender

"For it is when you surrender to the vulnerabilities of passion that you are fulfilled the most."
~David Shade

Get her to the point of total surrender, making her completely naked to you in every way: physically, emotionally, and spiritually.

Post Coital Re-Bonding

"Every true lover knows that the moment of greatest satisfaction comes when ecstasy is long over, and he beholds before him the flower which has blossomed beneath his touch."
~Don Juan DeMarco

After an emotionally powerful sexual experience, you MUST ground her again. You must make her feel close to you and secure with you. You must demonstrate to her how very important she is to you and how much you appreciate her. You must re-establish that emotional connection and intimacy.

This prevents her from later feeling sleazy and cheap, it makes her become even closer to you, and it makes her look forward to the next episode even more.

The Ultimate Sex Toy to Unleash Her Inner Animal

The Remote Control Egg is an egg-shaped vibrator that is turned on and off by radio remote control. You hold the remote! It is a totally awesome way to demonstrate your dominance. Makes dining out most interesting.

You can read a story on my blog of how I have used the remote control egg:

DavidShadesBlog.com

SECTION 3

Success Stories

CHAPTER 18
THE BEST SEX I EVER HAD
MASTERFUL LOVER SUCCESS STORIES FROM AROUND THE WORLD

"When you know how to truly please a woman, you won't have any problem getting women, your problem will be keeping them at arm's length."
~Mark Cunningham

Contained below are a number of e-mails that I have received from clients. Here is an e-mail from Samantha in Arizona:

Dear David, Thank you so much for your techniques.

My husband is a very passionate lover, he has always had the good guy, bad boy personality. Outside the bedroom he treats me like a princess, making me feel safe and secure, making sure I want for nothing, but in the bedroom, I can let go and be free, he lets me be the good girl gone bad, and I can't seem to get enough of him.

The way he takes control of my body, touching and moving me. I feel secure and wild at the same time. He has always made it his OWN personal pleasure to make sure I'm pleased well beyond measure, before he is.

He is the greatest lover I've ever had. Sometimes we have sex 3 or 4 times a day with multiple orgasms each time.

I want to personally thank you for your technique the DEEP SPOT, we tried it and WOW WOW WOOOW.

He is always looking for ways to improve our sex life, and every time is different from the last. If more guys knew what my husband knew there would be no infidelity problems anywhere.

Oh and by the way we're not new at this love game we've been married for ten wonderful years, and it's always been like this from the beginning. He never let the newness wear off because the way he makes love to me each time is like the first time. I can't get enough, he leaves me looking forward to the next time always.

Once again thank you for all your techniques, while my husband had most of these down pat already, there were some new one for us to try out. Please keep on teaching men how to please their women. Pleasure and passion from my husband has carried us through some pretty rough times.

Here is an e-mail from Stephanie in California:

David,

I just wanted to let you know that I have purchased your material, read it, and then read it again. I also gave this to the guy that I am currently seeing and WOW!!! Nough said.

He is not only trying everything you say, I have also learned a lot about my own sexuality. I own my own business and I am a very confident women. However, you taught me that the feelings I had about wanting to be a slut in the bedroom are totally natural. I know that your material is geared toward the

guys, but I have also learned how to be a
Masterful Lover for my man. THANK YOU THANK
YOU THANK YOU!!

Here is an e-mail from Karynia in Australia:

I always have great admiration for men who
are dedicated to women's pleasure and I
truly love that you have made it your
mission in life to help more men achieve
this.

"Give Women Screaming Orgasm's" certainly
delivers what it promises! I'm surprised you
haven't heard me already! My lovely
boyfriend put the CDs straight into his car
and has been listening to them and putting
the information into action with wonderful
results.

We already have an incredible love life,
but we've both learned a lot already and as
we put more of the techniques into action I
can see things are going to keep getting
even better. I've also spread the word about
how amazing the information is to lots of
friends, family, colleagues and anyone else
who'll listen. I'm sure they'll be putting
in their orders soon. Every man NEEDS your
information!

As a very sexual and passionate woman I am
truly grateful to you. In fact, I would love
to see you receive a Nobel Peace Prize one
day. I really believe it's possible. Don't
underestimate the magnitude of your gift to
the world!

Thank you so much.

Yours faithfully,

Karynia

Here is an e-mail from Denise in Pennsylvania:

Hi David! I just want to thank you for everything. My boyfriend and I are head over heels in love, so when it comes to the bedroom (or bathroom or kitchen, pretty much anywhere) he is AMAZING! He recently told me about his fantasy of making me squirt, which I was completely unaware of. I mean, I'm 29 and I've had lots of sex, but squirting orgasms? I had no idea!

He and I practiced until finally I got good at it. He made me squirt four times in a row! He is so attentive and genuinely wants to make sure I feel as good as possible. WOW, I'm a lucky woman!

We're total freaks in bed and because he's sooooo good to me, I give him a little prize, which is coming in my butt! He loves it and truthfully, I like it too! He and I will try anything in bed, we're that comfortable, so if you have any fun ideas... please let me know! I think your material is amazing David! Thank you so much for caring, because, trust me, great sex is key to having a wonderful relationship!

She squirts and scores in PA,

Denise :)

Here is an e-mail from Jenna in Atlanta:

Hi David,

There is no doubt in my mind that EVERY man worth his salt should read and implement your guides. Personally, I have never read anything except what's in these delicious emails and what's on your website. I forward your emails to my whomever my current lover is, if they ignore it, I break up with them pretty fast. If however they act on the information, they get to stay around and bless me with all they have learned.

I am engaged now to the man who took it seriously. He rocks my world and we have found that I wear him out and yet he continues to bring me one wild orgasm after another even after he is spent. He has no need to hypnotize me as I want to experience everything life has to offer with him. We have done threesomes and intend to experiment with many other "taboos". In return for his generous and masterful loving, I strive to be a woman worthy of him.

Truth be told I will not settle for less than a masterful lover. All men should strive to be one and hence climb the ladder of survival from a beta male to a virile alpha male... grrrr.

Thank You and Take Care David,

Jenna

40 in Atlanta, GA

Here is an e-mail from Wendy:

I am a 49 year old woman involved with a 55 year old man. The first after my 22 year marriage ended. We have amazing sex. He brings me to orgasm which is something I didn't always have with my ex-husband.

But when I read your emails, it is all about pleasing the woman. This is just such an odd thing to me. When I was married, it was all about making sure he was pleased. I didn't worry about faking as long as he was pleasured.

With my new man, I want to do anything that will please him. Is that it? He makes me so satisfied that I want me keep making him happy. Like, the more we do it, the more we want to do it. That's why your books give men the power to make women want it? Is this that simplistic? I know that respect is number one in a relationship and I have that finally. Is my sex that good because I respect him more than I ever respected my ex?

By the way, reading your material makes me realize something that I didn't feel in my marriage-I am a sensuous, extremely sexy woman in the prime of her life! Wanting sex is so new to me! Thank you for making me realize that sex can be fantastic!

Wendy

Here is an e-mail from Tammy, a Navy wife in San Diego, California:

My story is really kind of simple. My husband and I had a very routine sex life... always missionary and never anything new and a lot of it was because of my confidence about myself. I have had 2 kids in the last 2 1/2 years and my sex drive was way down.

Well, my husband who is deployed, came home on leave a few weeks ago and told me there was some new things he wanted to try on me. Let me tell you, I have never really been vocal in bed and wow that changed. Every single time we had sex while he was home I was having multiple orgasms and the great part about it too was that since he knew I was enjoying it so much he had more than 1 orgasm too on a few occasions. I was begging him to do more and we couldn't help ourselves on doing things where I normally wouldn't agree to doing it.

Wow now I cannot wait until he comes home again so we can start where we left off and my husband is very excited too. Thanks again David... this really helped our sex life a great deal.

Tammy

Here is an e-mail from Barbara:

Hello David,

I purchased your book, The Secrets Of Female Sexuality. WOW. You know exactly what a woman wants and how it starts in the mind.

I could never get my ex-husband to understand how he talked to me made a big difference on my responsiveness in the bedroom (or any room). He didn't command the respect or trust. We were married for 23 years. Too long for an orgasm-less relationship.

I'm 53 now and for the first time in my life, I feel like a real woman. The man I'm having a relationship with now is a true masterful lover. He has brought out the tigress in me and keeps me wanting more and more. I can't get enough of him. He also can't get enough of me. He can make me cum just reading his emails, fully clothed, without even touching myself. His words get me all wet. He also told me he gets a hard on just thinking about me.

We are so playful together, just like kids. It is amazing. This past year I have felt younger and more alive than I did 20 years ago.

Thank you David

Here is an e-mail from Michael in Curacao, Netherlands

David,

This is going to sound like the 'old broken record', but I'm going to say it anyways,...YOU'RE THE FVCKING MAN.... Period!!!

During the last few years I have bought quite a lot of your products as I was seriously looking for ways to try to better my life and hopefully save my failing marriage. But I was too scared to put them to use as I didn't know where and how to start. So about a year ago my (now ex-) wife divorced my ass.

For about three months now I've been dating this beautiful (also divorced) woman, who's a daddy's girl, has some high levels of self esteem and works as a teacher. And with her I finally found the courage to be the man, assert myself as a person with a path in life which I intend to walk.. period... and best of all, put those lessons of yours to some good use.

We really took our time to get to know each other better and work on our communication, and not worry so much about sex.

But last night was the second time we had sex and boy it surprised me!!! On the first occasion, I worked on awakening her vagina using your deep spot technique (which gave her her vaginal orgasm by the way), introducing dirty talk a la Hot Phone S.x and tease her (a lot) with that welcomed method technique!!!

This woman is sooo responsive to me that after a just few minutes of some heavy french kissing, she's literally dripping wet...Sooo wet that I didn't need the astro glide to do the welcomed method.

So last night it turns out that after all that prep work, she had her first squirting vaginal orgasm. And after a few more seconds of thrusting inside her, she had her second squirting vaginal orgasm...and after a minute or so of thrusting...she had her third...DAMN...I was on a roll here... sooo...I kept going... ;-)

After her fifth, she breathlessly said that she wanted a break...to be able to breath. And with that she asked me if I came...which made me realize that I was so concentrated on her pleasure that I literally forgot about my own. I was having way too much fun with her. And I didn't feel like I was going to come any time soon.

So you know what I did? While she had her sixth squirting vaginal orgasm,.... I FAKED my own!!!

Never in my entire 39 years alive would I have thought the day will come that I would fake my orgasm. And I don't know if you can agree with me here....but I didn't care whether I came or not. It felt soooo good to see that beautiful creature almost pass out with pleasure, that even though I didn't come, I felt way more satisfied than I ever was.

The last few days she's been all over me. Trying to make sure I have everything I want, especially in the food department. And she keeps asking me why she's behaving like that with me...ha ha!!!

I'm reading my manuals (Secrets of Female Sexuality and GWWSO) everyday like a menu bit by bit and listen to the cd's any time I have a chance over and over again to make that knowledge part of my natural system.

Thanks man, you literally changed my life...for the (fvcking) best!!!

Michael L.

Here is an e-mail from Michael in Los Angeles:

Mr. Shade,

Thanks to you, my life has changed for the better, not only that, but so have the lives of wonderful women in my life. Your programs are stellar. If anyone has any doubts about them, let me be the thousandth person to say that those doubts are unfounded and should be thrown out the window.

I'm 27, have been dating women older than I, who have had much more sexual experience than me. Not just more partners, but they've had all sorts of experiences, including threesomes (with both two women and two men). Up until a few months ago, this would have intimidated me. But after reading your books and recently purchasing your ASH program, things have changed.

These "experienced" women tell me that they've never had anyone like me before in there lives. Someone who respects them and knows how to truly please them like no one has before.

On many occasions, I've heard that the women I were seeing had either no vaginal orgasms or maybe two in her ENTIRE lifetime, and it was from digital stimulation. With me they have at least three intense vaginal orgasms in ONE night. Just last night, the woman in my life and I shared the most amazing simultaneous orgasms that she still felt throughout her body for hours afterwards. She's never had this before, she couldn't stop smiling the whole time afterwards and telling me that I was her best lover ever, she was THAT happy and satisfied.

It's truly amazing and a wonderful feeling to help women open up, feel connected, and know they can have the most amazing orgasms. All the women in my life are really happy now that they've found a "Masterful-Lover". They've changed, everything in their lives seems so much brighter. Even their friends notice it on them. After years of being in abusive or un-satisfying relationships, someone has come along and shown them that a REAL man who they can trust and respect, who respects them, and who they can share the most amazing sexual experiences with, do exist. I have women traveling from all parts of the world to see me now. All this change in just a few months.

To ANYONE who thinks your programs are disrespectful to women...this program is ALL about respecting women and making them feel spectacular. Making them feel like they've never felt before.

There are many benefits for both men and women when studying your programs. Just a small benefit that I've had is all the free dinners, trips, etc..that I'm now receiving simply because the women in my life can't have enough and want to PLEASE me any way possible because it makes THEM happy, and I'm always happy to oblige in any way to make them happy. Once again, let me emphasize that this is all about respect for both sexes and making everyone happy. This is not about personal power over someone else, but helping your woman and you both feel great and truly connected.

Thank you Mr. Shade. I truly wish you much success and happiness in your life, for you and yours. It's the least you deserve from all the women and men that you've helped.

Here's hoping you're enjoying your weekend as much as I am...

Ciao, Michael

Here is an e-mail from Dave in Canada:

I recently bought and read "The Secrets Of Female Sexuality" and "Give women Wild Screaming Orgasms". I must say it's changed me and taught me a lot.

Before getting your books, I had acquainted myself with one of the most attractive women I have ever met. She's talented in arts, successful professionally, an accomplished and elite athlete, and a complete knockout. The guys at work nearly always talk about how hot she is.

I became interested in her and she reciprocated. We hung out a couple of times and were both attracted to each other and began having sex. She mentioned often that I was the best she ever had, but she had never had an orgasm, and thought that something was wrong with her.

As our relationship progressed, I became increasingly paranoid that she couldn't like me. I constantly wondered when she was going to call me and call the whole thing off. (She did at one point, but came back later and I of course just took her back immediately, no questions asked).

When we were together I was always afraid of leading her, making the first move, being assertive, and just being a man in general. I was constantly indecisive, always wondering if she was happy, never suggesting anything specific because I was so damned intimidated. I started trying to prove myself to her by always saying things that I thought would impress her, or make myself seem worthy.

Then she started saying she'd call me later and wouldn't. She'd show up sometimes 45 minutes late for a date and didn't seem to care. I was always "okay" with that, though it made me feel shitty.

We agreed to see a movie one day, and despite my constant txting her, she never responded or showed up. When we saw each other at work the following week I pretended like it was no big deal... I think you get the picture.

Then I read your books and realized that I wasn't being a man. My subconscious was sabotaging the entire relationship because it deemed myself unworthy of her.

I started remapping my subconscious world through some techniques I learned in a meditation class (I began to see my entire world differently) and in a week I knew what I had to do.

It was important for me to take responsibility for my actions and not be the victim. Though I wanted so badly to make her feel bad, blame her, and label her a disrespectful person, I admitted to myself that I wasn't getting respect because I firmly believed that I didn't deserve it. By taking responsibility I felt empowered to change my situation. No person is worth sacrificing your dignity, no matter how hot and perfect they are.

So I called her and said, in a nutshell, the whole thing wasn't working for me, that she's a really great person but that I needed to walk away from it because I wasn't being respected and I refuse to be in a situation like that. When she got defensive, I assured her that she's a good person, I held nothing against her and didn't blame her one bit for what happened. I felt liberated and strong.

That afternoon she asked me to meet her to chat for drinks, which I accepted. David, she started looking at me differently. Her eyes sparkled and she hung on my every word. She was really open and expressive to me. We decided to get together the next day, and she was constantly keeping me up to date on where she was at, and whether she was running a bit behind.

That evening she came over and had her first orgasm (deep spot method). Then I lead her to another. We ran out of time to go for a third, but I felt so empowered that given the time, and evening of constant orgasms seemed imminent.

As I held her after the second, she laid there staring at me and gazing at the ceiling in disbelief (I was amazed too). I gave this perfect 10 hottie an unforgettable experience that no one could do before me. I not only feel lucky, but that she's lucky to have a strong man unafraid to lead her in a proper way.

I understand what this woman (and any other woman) wants and needs. I'm willing to walk away from any situation that isn't in line with my self-concept, including this woman who I totally adore.

I want to reiterate how important self-esteem is. If you don't respect yourself, if you're desperate, afraid of being a man with confidence, nothing will work.

You can't have the unassuming, strong yet not overbearing confidence that women desire without an unwavering belief in yourself as a person that deserves all the right things. This was a powerful lesson for me David.

Thank you.

Here is an e-mail from Robert in Cambridge, Massachusetts:

I have your "David Shade's Manual" and I've found it very helpful, as are these newsletters that you send out. The first step is always realizing that something is possible, and then all kinds of amazing things happen.

I am currently seeing a woman who has been blessed with some phenomenal gifts, and just KNOWING that things like extended orgasms are possible (and listening to your interview and reading your book and following your advice) has allowed me to give her orgasms that have lasted close to 10 minutes (clitoral with oral and digital stimulation). Your latest newsletter encouraged me to try some post-coital suggestion, which has done wonders as well.

Nothing breeds success like success. So now, after she has achieved incredible pleasure in ways that she never thought possible, I have convinced her that everything is possible and that it WILL happen. She has now started to experience extended vaginal orgasms as well. She now routinely has 5 or 6 orgasms per session, she can have orgasms clitorally and vaginally, and, suffice it to say, she is a very happy girl.

One of the most powerful things I've gotten from the whole experience is that women want to be led and if 'I' believe something can happen, then I can make it her reality as well--and truly, I learned that from you. Hopefully there is something in my e-mail that might let others believe that it is not something that only David Shade can make happen.

The other incredibly powerful thing I got from you is the idea that you have to know how to ravish a woman--I think it's in your primer about what women want.

David, this girl knows that I am simply going to take her whenever and wherever I choose -- and she loves it.

Now, in the past, I would have been way too timid to ever think I could get away with something like that--thinking that I might upset her, or seem too much of a jerk, that I might only want her for sex, etc, etc, etc.

With this girl, one night early in our relationship after I'd given her the first extended orgasm she'd ever had (it was maybe 30 seconds at the time), I told her, "Look, we seem to be getting along really well, so, just to be honest with you, I want you to realize this from the beginning, but I am going to ravish you constantly. I am going to fuck you as often as I want and wherever I want, and I'm not going to stop. I'll know when you REALLY don't want to, but in general, I'm going to just take you as I please. This is the way I am, and I'm not going to change, so if you think that's going to bother you, I want to give you the option now to leave."

Of course, I half expected her to get upset or to equivocate or somehow try and take some of that power back. Instead, she broke into the biggest smile and literally screamed, "Baby, do you really mean it! I mean, really, you're not just saying that?" Of course, I truly spoke from the heart and told her that was the way that I am -- and when I wanted her, I was simply going to take her. She was so happy.

So, of course, I have. David, I literally fuck this girl every single time I want. She'll be cooking breakfast and she'll know I'm looking at her ass -- because I'll tell her flat out. Then I'll say something like "you'll be lucky if you get to finish that omelet before I fuck you". She'll giggle and get a little scared, but also very, very excited. Then, at some point, I will just go up to her, roughly yank her robe apart (or her panties down, or pull her skirt up -- this has happened quite a bit), bend her over the stove and take her right there. David, she LOVES it.

Even when she says she doesn't want to have sex (she doesn't like to immediately after eating a big meal), if I feel like it, I will tell her, "I don't care," and I will slowly, slowly, slowly unbuckle my pants and take them off and walk towards her. Initially she runs, and I just walk slowly behind her and follow her. Of course, before too long she can't wait for me to catch her and bend her over whatever piece of furniture happens to be close by. At this point, she usually has her first vaginal orgasm within 30 seconds, her second within another minute or two and she will always have a third when she can feel that I'm getting ready to cum.

The point is, David, I am having the most incredible sex, as often as I want, and of course, I am giving her the best sex of her life and she can't get enough. Do you want to know the one thing she always asks me? She'll look at me after I've just taken her, or given her an orgasm over the phone, or told her that I was going to fuck her in her office, or anytime I am direct and tell her what I'm going to do? She looks at me expectantly and asks, "You're never going to change, right? This isn't some sort of trick? You'll always be this way, right?"

She had two orgasms the other night before I even got in her all the way. I just stuck the head in and let it sit there and she had two - just from the head.

This is, of course, a hot girl that is used to having men pursue her and wine and dine her, take her on private airplanes to movie premiers, etc, etc, etc. She used to work as a bartender in NYC, so she knows all the moves. Now she spends all her money to come and see me, blows off her friends and family and just wants to come here on the weekends and let me fuck her all day long.

Her favorite place for me to take her -- the grocery store, because then she knows that we're going to stay in and she'll get more time in bed. Dude, I'm fucking serious. Her favorite place to go -- our "date" place is the grocery store.

On the weekends, I generally fuck her at least 3 times a day and she usually has at least 3 or 4 orgasms every time. Seriously, I don't think there has been a day in the

last two months where she has had less than
15 orgasms in one day. Sometimes, when I'm
feeling rowdy, I'll put her in a position
that I know she can't help but have orgasms
in (hitting the deep spot) and make her
continue to have orgasms until she begs me
to stop.

The only bad part about all of this is
that she really doesn't have anyone she can
share this with. None of her friends would
believe that she has continuous orgasms that
last 15 minutes or more, none of them would
believe that she had over 20 orgasms in one
day--so she feels a little frustrated that
she can't actually share this with anyone.

Still, truth be told, she was ready for
this when I found her. She just needed
someone to lead her--and truthfully, it's
been very easy. She fits the profile you
indicated about being a Daddy's girl and
highly intelligent (she's a Mensa chick), so
you were right on the money about making
sure you choose the right one.

David-this is all from post-coital
suggestion and making her believe that
everything I say is going to happen WILL
happen, and then it does.

Next I'm going to work on making her cum
as soon as I put my dick in her and then the
"orgasm on command".

David, life is good. Life is oh, so
fucking incredibly good.

Thanks for showing us the way.

Robert, you chose wisely, and you were man enough to bring
out the woman in her.

Some readers may be taken aback by some of the things you
said to her, such as, "I am going to fuck you as often as I want and

wherever I want," but it was said in the specific context of respect, enhancement of the relationship you two share together, a celebration of her sexuality, and understanding the fact that she loves to be a woman. This is evident in her reply, which was basically, "Promise?"

Here is an e-mail from Michael in San Francisco:

David,

I wanted to express my appreciation for your materials and insights.

I was always a good lover. Women who had never had an orgasm during intercourse would do so with me, but your material has moved my ability to help a woman unleash her sexuality to an entirely new level. It is like a miracle to see women open up sexually to a place they never dreamed, but always hoped, they could go.

If there is a downside to being a masterful lover, its that ending relationships can be really hard. Women get incredibly attached to the person who broke down those walls for them and took charge of their pleasure, holding their hand through the anxieties that come with defying social mores.

I write today only because I felt a note of appreciation was necessary, for me. The leap from good lover to a masterful lover is a leap of faith. Even with the knowledge that a woman will come from the sound of your voice, it takes a leap of faith predicated on believing in your message, your material, and one's self. So thanks for helping me make that leap.

Two years ago, I would have not believed that I would be telling a beautiful, successful woman to "Shut up. You will come when I tell you." And I certainly would have found it hard to believe that this woman would wait patiently, looking adoringly at me, for her permission to come. And it would have defied imagination that she was going to come when I told her and begged me to let it stop because she will not stop her orgasms without my permission.

I dont even need to touch this woman anymore. Last night, I laid her on her back on the couch, and narrated her getting fucked. She came so hard that I was concerned that her couch would never dry. Later I instructed her to come while she was sucking me, and she kept coming for 4 minutes on her knees. She not only squirts, she drowns things and my laundry bill is impressive these days.

Sometimes I narrate more tender fantasies, sometimes more fantastic. She loves them all. Last night she greeted me at the gate to her garden, leading to her apartment, in panties and high heels. There is a long walk past the street, but she didn't care. This is a woman who attended Bible college. She has been transformed by the attention and the unlocking of her sexuality. She will never be the same and this pleases me beyond measure. She seems more complete and happy as a woman now.

So thank you.

Michael

Here is an e-mail from Eric in Colorado:

I'm an older gent and bought your materials after I got divorced. I want your readers to know that your materials work for ALL AGES. In fact, the great sex they're learning now can be theirs for as long as they live.

I'm 55, old enough to be many of their dads. I've dated many women in their early 40s, but took a chance and dated a woman OLDER than me who is hotter than many 20 year olds. (I know... many readers may not believe ANYONE over 50 can be hot, but they just haven't lived long enough.) Anyway, some details: She has high self-esteem and is a law-enforcement professional. She is reserved, traditional, and very proper in public. I also treat her like a queen in public.

In private, though, she loves kissing and fucking for hours, but she didn't know that until AFTER she met me. Her previous men were ignorant lovers. Sex was so-so to her. BTW, she is very cute, has a tight ass and slim body from working out for 20 years, and has 36D breasts that love my kisses. Many 20 year old girls could only HOPE to look as good as her when they turn 30, much less past 50.

When we started getting intimate, I told her my goal was her Extreme Pleasure. She just smiled, but now she's a true believer. She wants to have sex with me every night (yes...EVERY night). We also play sex games together. She says every time with me is a challenge and is different for her. Every morning, while I'm still sleeping she strokes my cock to make me hard so she can "start the day right". BTW, she also became a squirter (we need lots of towels on the bed.)

She calls me her "boy toy" and I call her my "sex wench." When we travel in the car, the favorite place to rest her hand is on my cock. In a restaurant, she typically puts a wide napkin on my lap so she can hide her hand under it and stroke me. Now, get this, although I have a fit physique, I am only of average looks and an average sized cock. It's how I learned to treat her that made all the difference.

Thanks for your help, Eric

Here is an e-mail from George in Bulgaria:

I am 25 and I had so little experience that I considered myself a virgin. So I started learning about women and pick-up. That gave me some confidence but I felt it wasn't enough. Until I came to you.

When I met my girl she told me about her experience, and to be honest I felt a bit intimidated. She had far richer experience than I. She told me that she had had only two orgasms - one clitoral and she wasn't sure what the other was. Though I felt self-doubt, I knew that I knew stuff none of my male friends knew about women. That gave me confidence stronger than my fear.

What I did first was to play with her deep spot and G-spot, and YES - I gave her her first vaginal orgasms! Man, was she grateful! She turned into this wonderful sexual creature that had "screaming orgasms" every time we had sex. She even calls me "Lord of the Fingers" from time to time. At first I thought, "What the fuck?!" I felt like THE MAN.

Now, about last week. She came to stay with me for the holiday week. You say it is important to use dirty talk, so I decided to try it. I didn't know what the response would be. So during sex I just told her, "You love when I fuck you like that, don't you?" It was like she was WAITING to hear that. "I love when we have sex this way" was replaced by "I love when you fuck me really hard from behind". (She loves the doggy style position, which she first tried with me.) Now she says "have sex" less often than "you fucking me". Once she said that she wants me to tie her hands and "rape" her, and once "I've never been fucked that good before". It's like I opened the floodgates of her sexuality.

For the last 4 or 5 days I felt like I was living in a porn movie. She was doing things she'd never done before, she was jumping on me and ASKING me to "fuck her hard" while I was reading a book or watching TV or she sat on my leg and started humping it.

I know that there are men who ask their partners whether they came during sex. If I ask my girl it won't be "whether" but "how many this time".

Once I was stimulating her clit, using your Welcomed Method. It became so sensitive that I was only gently rubbing the shaft and she came powerfully. She said she felt "little needles" all over her body, even on her face. From then on every orgasm was AT LEAST that powerful, and she squirts every time! Once she said she came four times during the foreplay alone.

She told me that sometimes I turn her on just by looking at her. One time we were watching TV, my leg was next to hers and I was moving it up and down unconsciously thus rubbing hers lightly. She turned and just said, "Stop it, you're turning me on."

The techniques I use - ONLY G-spot and deep spot stimulation and sometimes clitoral. Really, just that. More important though is the mindset I've developed. I TELL her what to do and she loves it, I LEAD her and she loves it, I call her "my little slut" and she loves it.

When she has an orgasm and squirts I comfort her by telling her, "That's my girl," or, "Good girl." Most of all I LOVE caressing, hugging and kissing her after her orgasms. I LOVE to do that. It's a wonderful feeling seeing her so satisfied and so happy while she is in a trance-like state or smiling or giggling or crying trying to wind her body around mine like a snake or trying to touch every part of my body.

There were times when I came 3 minutes after sticking it in but now I feel like I can control when I come and I don't care if I come or not, really!

I realize that for many guys this will seem like I made it up and I didn't quite believe it at first... but it is true. I even don't have time now to describe everything thoroughly!

P.S. Are all women like that or did my girl just turn out to be hypersexual? David, after you, picking up girls seems like child's play.

Thank you for the person you are and for what you do!

You truly change men's lives, mine for sure!

Such fantastic success from simple techniques, dirty talk, and the right mind set.

Here is an e-mail from Russell in Indiana:

I'll start with my experience before reading your books. I knew only what I had seen in the movies, as far as how to have sex. Then I met a very experienced girl (a stripper) and she taught me a lot about how to make a woman feel good, and she enjoyed everything. I had a lot of fun with her.

Then I met my future ex wife. She was also very experienced, but she had never had an orgasm. I thought I knew a lot about women, and I told her I thought I could give her one, so I tried doing oral but it just tickled her. I pretty much tried everything. Then we bought her a vibrator and she had her first orgasm. It was neat to see the look on her face. She was actually able to have many orgasms with this vibrator, so that's how we had sex every time.

I actually gave up on trying to give her one without it. I just thought that was the only way she could have one. So 5 years and 2 kids later, she left me and we divorced. It crushed me beyond belief. I know you know what it's like, but the difference was she got the kids and wouldn't let me see them.

After 6 months of feeling sorry for myself and hardly talking to her, I decided to e-mail her and we started talking. In one of her e-mails, she was being a bitch and told me that she had had orgasms with other guys without a vibrator. That really hit me in the gut. I asked her why she didn't tell me what she liked, or what felt good, so that I could do that. I, like every other guy, don't what to be considered lame in bed.

So I began my research and started reading everything I could on sex and giving a woman an orgasm. I wasn't really learning anything until I came across David Shade's "Give Women Wild Screaming Orgasms". I want to say God bless you for writing these books. I studied it over and over. Now I felt like I really knew something.

I bought your other two e-books also, and I'm still studying them. It really has boosted my confidence, and I'm a lot less shy around new women, where before I would hardly say hello to them.

I also found a woman who is worthy of being with me. She was the second one I got to use my newfound knowledge on. The first time we had sex I could tell I had blown her mind, and it made her pussy sore from having so many orgasms (4). She has been up for pretty much anything since that first night of having sex.

She didn't like giving BJs and she didn't want anything to do with anal, but after reading your "Manual" and giving her many, many orgasms, she let me do anal on her. At first she said it hurt really badly, but I told her, "I know baby, but you like it; you like the feeling of me being inside your ass." A few moments later, after more dirty talk, she had one of her most powerful orgasms. She was dripping from her pussy. We did it 3 more times that night and every night for about a week.

I also started planting other seeds in her head. I used your "Now She Loves To Go Down" chapter from your Manual. She never even liked giving head at all, and before I knew it, she was giving me head all the time. I would always plant seeds in her mind about how she liked sucking my big cock, and how it turned her on. Then one night she kept on going with it (before she would do it only for a few minutes). I told her I was going to cum. She swallowed it all, even squeezed out everything, licked her lips, and said it tasted good.

I couldn't believe it. Giving women pleasure is the most fun I could have imagined, and she tries to make sure that I get what I want and that I feel good. I love it.

She is up for anything. I haven't gotten as far as the hypnosis yet, but I look forward to it, and she does too.

I want to thank you again, David. You have really helped me beyond belief. Keep everything up, and I look forward to any more books you write. I'll be your customer for life, and I recommend your books to all of my friends.

There is a tremendous amount of pent-up sexual potential in a woman, and men need to understand the immense amount of power that men have because only a man can release that potential in a woman.

That requires BEing a Man. A man who can drive like a man. A man who can lead. A man who adores everything about her that defines her as a woman. A man who revels in bringing out the ruthlessly expressive, decedent, primal, carnal, insatiably hungry, natural woman in her.

Here is an e-mail from Bob in Palo Alto, California:

Unleashing the raging sexuality in a shy, incredibly sexy, virgin daddy's girl:

When I met David Shade about 3 years ago he immediately struck me as being a personally powerful man. When he spoke, it was with an authoritative tone that said, "I know what I'm talking about, and if you truly want to go down the path, I can show you the way." On the other hand, I was a selfish kid with little experience with women and had no idea what much of what he said meant at the time. I say selfish because deep down I wanted to learn how to seduce and sleep with attractive women for my own self-validation, which I didn't have from any other sources. He will show you the path, but you must walk down it.

Looking back, I remember sitting over coffee, or lunch, and he'd put questions to me like, "What is it that you really want?" "What if you had exactly what it is you wanted? How would that be for you?" "Why would a beautiful woman want to sleep with you?" "Why do you want to fuck hot women? What would be true for you?" I kept thinking, "Why wouldn't my mentor give me a straight answer? Why was everything he said so cryptic to me at the time?" Still, I thought about what he said a lot. He was testing me. Testing my character and my ability to think for myself.

Through spending time with David, I soon began picking up pieces of his belief system, a little bit at a time. I learned from listening to him and watching him work in the real world about being a personally powerful man.

I learned firsthand what he is talking about when he says "self-respect above all else". I learned about how women are amazingly sexual creatures, and how the amount of potential in a woman's raw sexuality is beyond what most men will ever know. The right women of course. High self-esteem women. I learned about how low self-esteem women will actually not allow themselves to be completely sexually aware, because they feel they don't deserve it. I also learned that the high self-esteem women are the ones with the most potential, because deep down locked inside them is a box full of amazing sexuality and dreams and passions. David gives you the keys to unlock that box.

I stopped worrying so much about sleeping with women for my own selfish gratification, and started wondering about how hard I could make that hot girl in line at the store come if I took her home. I started wondering if she was capable of letting me show her more about her own body than she knows is possible... I started wondering about giving her the gift of unlocking her box of sexual fantasy and pleasure. In short, I really started appreciating the sexuality of women a lot more. I learned that you can never make a woman have sex with you. You can never convince her, and if you do, she won't be enjoying it and is doing it out of guilt. What if she was in the state of mind to WANT to give you the most amazing pleasure of your life... what if she was in the state of mind to give you full access to her body because you can make her feel better than anybody else? What if she genuinely wanted to give to you everything possible, because you give her ground-shaking orgasms every time you are together?

So, I went and found my current girlfriend. I'll save you all the pickup stuff. There are plenty of guys out there that will teach you the arts of pickup. This will focus on what to do after you HAVE the girl. When we first met, she was a shy daddy's girl...incredibly sexy. This is the kind of girl that when you are walking down the street with her on your arm, other guys look, and they look often.

She was a virgin when we met, and really had no sexual experience. When I first kissed her she couldn't even kiss me back with any sort of intensity because she was so shy and nervous...She would just blush and giggle and slowly kiss me back, yet she liked kissing me...With my newfound belief systems I learned from David Shade I thought...how wonderful! She's never even had the misfortune of being with a self-validating, one-pump chump, and I want to make her come so hard that she shakes before I even give myself to her! She was very, very shy, but through our conversations I could see she was very high self-esteem. She was very intelligent, she was very close to her parents, she cared about ambitions and goals in life. The more we talked the more I started to see her sexual potential in her words... The closer we got, the more our talk evolved into some of her sexual fantasies.

Here was a beautiful, amazing, sexual girl, yet it was all trapped inside her, and she was sitting waiting for a man to come along and show her how to let it all out.

I started with some basic things on the phone...First I would let her describe an ideal sexual situation--ones she'd fantasized about since she was a teenager...Then I would tell her, "Mmmm baby I love how wet your little pussy gets for me," as I heard her moaning into the phone with pleasure. I started getting her to imagine these situations so vividly that she'd have orgasms on the phone with me. There were a few times when we'd get together and I'd only take it so far with her--up to the points I had described to her and let her already imagine...Then I'd let her imagine going further, and after she could vividly imagine that I would physically take her further, I'd say, "Can you see that in the picture baby? Can you look down and see that hard cock sliding in your pussy?" Once somebody visualizes something in their mind it is much more real to them.

Soon she was having powerful orgasms for me and telling me how good she came. She also became much more verbal with ME...She started telling me how bad she wanted to do all these things to me, and would describe them to me in great detail for me.

David taught me what women really want: They want to be treated with dignity and respect--when they are around other people in the world and out and about...but she wants more than anything in this world to let that raging sexuality out of her and have her man fuck her like a naughty little slut when she is in the bedroom with him. Good sex to a woman is the physical manifestation of an incredible emotional bond with the man she loves.

I started telling her how I love that she is such a nice proper good girl around everybody else...mmmm, but when you are with me, you can be a naughty little girl, can't you? She would say, "Oh yes... I love being your naughty girl, but only yours!!!"

When we did actually get intimate the first time, all the talk and preparing her mind paid off--big time. First, I started with foreplay and touching her all over until I could feel her pussy dripping wet for me. Then, I used David's techniques mentioned in his "Give Women Wild Screaming

Orgasms" book on giving oral sex to your woman. If you don't know the anatomy of a woman's sexual organs you are really doing yourself a disservice in not having David's book! First I licked her clit steadily with my tongue until she had her first orgasm, then I licked her clit and gave her the deep spot at the same time, which drove her completely insane!!! I also used variations of other things in the "Give Women Wild Screaming Orgasms" book, like the hummer. I was in wonder lying there licking her clit, pushing my finger into her and giving her the deep spot and seeing how amazingly sexual my woman could be, and how I was unlocking her box right in front of me. She moaned, "Oh god oh god oh yes oh yes, I'm cuming for you!!! "

I realized at that moment there is nothing quite as rewarding as hearing your woman moan with intense pleasure and looking up at her face after she came so hard for you that her legs are quivering and seeing a big smile on her face. After that, she practically begged me to fuck her, which I did until she came again, soaking our bed sheets from her wetness by this point. I whisper in her ear how good her little pussy makes me feel when I fuck her, and tell her how she is MY girl, and I love how nasty she can be with only me. The more I intensify those feelings the wetter she gets, and the harder she gets off for me. It really is quite staggering.

These days our relationship couldn't be better. I am exploring new things with her sexually all the time, and she loves every bit of it. Guys, once you give your woman incredible pleasure like she has only dreamed of, she will want nothing more in this world than to make her man so happy and for him to come for her over and over again. Do what David tells you, be the man, learn about how to give your woman incredible pleasure because you love women, you adore women, and you are fascinated by their sexual capability...Then give it to them, and I assure you, your end will be taken care of. One of a woman's biggest turn-ons is how she can make the man she loves feel sooooo good, and she will want nothing more than to do that for you after you enlighten her in ways that David teaches you how to do.

Today my girlfriend told me how much she is looking forward to exploring all of her naughty little sexual fantasies with me, and wondered if I'd mind her learning them with me.:) I reward her good behavior now with things that she TRULY WANTS to do for me. When she tells me a sexual fantasy of hers I'll reward her by telling her that, yes, she's been a good girl for me and I will LET her enjoy those things. For instance, today she was telling me how she wants to try deep throating me while I lie back and enjoy it until I explode, and I said, "Mmmm yes baby I promise you that next time we are together, I will let you do that for me." When you are a sexually powerful man, and you show your woman pleasures that she's only had in her dreams, you will have full access to do anything you want to her, and you will have that access because she truly will long to experience those things with you.

When you learn David's material, your woman will beg you to do things to her that other men have to try and convince their women to do! I come all over her body because she asks me to now, I put my cock in her mouth, have her stick out her tongue and finish in her mouth...because she wants to make me feel so good--then she swallows every drop with a big smile on her face. I spank her and tell her how I love her to be my naughty little girl tonight, and she goes crazy and starts moaning. She already has a little list of positions she wants to try next time we're together. In short, when you take care of your woman the way she needs to be taken care of, she will literally obsess about you because that is what she has wanted whether she knows it or not since she was a little girl.

David Shade has been a profound influence on my way of thinking, and as a result a huge influence on my life. Let him show you the path, and then let yourself walk down it, and see for yourself the enjoyment of truly giving women incredible pleasure, and reaping the benefits of doing that for her!

Bob's success began at the beginning, when he chose wisely. Bob and his girlfriend are now married.

Find a woman who wants to enjoy everything that is woman, and then BE the Man.

Here is an e-mail from Randy:

I am writing to you so that I may share with you the success I have had with your Manual, and most importantly, thank you for being such a positive influence on my life.

I have wanted to write to you and express my thanks for all your help, but I was putting it off until I could write to you about succeeding in doing something that really caught my attention in your Manual.

I met a woman that passed the tests you taught me about being selective to find the "good ones".

We went out for some coffee at a place that I knew closed early (exit strategy if I did not like her, and reason to go back to my place if I did). We were back at my place in a bit under two hours, were kissing an hour after that, and she was having her first orgasm with me about an hour after that.

The interesting thing about this one is that her first two orgasms happened while she was fully clothed. The first orgasm left her with the most amazingly beautiful look of utter shock on her face! She kept saying, "How did you do that? Oh my god, how did you do that?"

At this point, she wanted to get fucked big time. She was pulling at my clothes, but I made sure to remove hers first, and then rub her clit briefly using a simplified version of the Welcomed Method. This drove her wild, and she said, "Oh my God, I can't even find it that fast!"

I wanted to be sure she would be vaginally orgasmic before having intercourse, so I got her close and then slid my finger inside her and rubbed the front of the Deep Spot. Boom! She came really hard!

I knew I had the green light at this point, so I gave her a moment to come to grips with all these new experiences, took the rest of my clothes off, worked her up with some sexy dirty talk, slapped on a condom, and with only the slightest bit of thrusting she came like crazy!

I was having some serious fun, so I went ahead and gave her a couple more, even though I had not ejaculated. She was not going to let me get away with that though, and so she rolled me over and went down on me. I know she was not validating herself by doing so. She truly wanted to reward me for helping her feel sexier than she had ever felt before, and since she was so wonderfully responsive in every way to me all night long, I was happy to show her how good I could come for her.

I decided to progressively train her, seeing her approximately one night a week so that she would have sufficient time to anticipate seeing me and drive her to fantasize about me.

The second night I started things off with two more Think-offs and then a nipple orgasm.

I then teasingly chastised her for fantasizing about me and showed her how she took "this hand" and "put it right here" and taught her to masturbate in front of me. We then had intercourse and I lost track of the number of orgasms.

The third night I did the Welcomed Method on her and taught her to relax into her orgasm and sustain it.

The fourth night I did the humming clit sucking and that of course worked wonderfully. She was fully convinced that anything I said would happen would, indeed, happen.

I did her doggy while holding her hair and talking dirty. I've always fantasized about doing a woman doggy, and any time that I did in real life, I would come almost instantly because it was such a powerful fantasy for me.

With the dirty talk, it puts my focus on the woman and her experience, which allows me to screw like crazy without getting overly focused on my own pleasure and ejaculating. Having a woman in orgasm while I did her doggy was like climbing Mt. Everest and finally making it to the summit; it was a huge success for me.

The next night I did a ten count to orgasm, and I was actually a little bit unsure how she would respond, but she didn't skip a beat and came right on ten!

It was a weekend, so she stayed the night and the next morning I woke her up with her on her stomach and some morning wood pressed against her ass. I get her turned on right away and she must have still been wet from the night before because I slid right in with very little foreplay. I told her to reach under and rub her clit while I fucked her. You know the results.

I constantly prove to her with my actions that I am fully vested in her pleasure and that I am also interested in ALL of her emotions. I do not rush getting to sex, I watch her to signal me, and then I will even slow her pace down to build anticipation. I usually make her talk to me after sex.

Also, I have never formally induced trance in her since she proved to be so highly suggestible from the very beginning. I decided that the experiences would be more powerful for her if she could not try to convince herself that she was having the experiences only because of hypnosis.

She eventually told me that before meeting me she had a difficult time even having one single orgasm during sex. I've been nurturing her fantasies and she told me that she used to masturbate to the imaginings of movie stars or men with no faces; never someone she knew. She now regularly fantasizes about me when she masturbates.

My lovely and willing love lab test subject was over at my house, but she was on her period. I could just tell that as much as she would prefer otherwise, she was expecting me to be inconsiderate of her situation and uninterested in her until her 'curse' had passed. I saw this as a big opportunity!

I knew she could orgasm without me even taking her clothes off, so I proved to her just how sexy she could remain (to me and to herself) even during that 'time of the month'. I did my little "magic trick", made her feel wonderful, and then explained to her that orgasms while menstruating massage her reproductive organs, helping to eliminate pain and cramping.

She hugged me tight and was taken with gratitude for me doing something entirely for her benefit. Of course, I did not tell her that it was part of a larger process that she was unknowingly going through. I wanted her to have an orgasm while sucking my cock.

Fast forward to one month later (last night) and she is on my couch, anticipating some affection. I've been developing her trust and responsiveness for some time now. I had held back Think-offs for a while, because I knew that I wanted to keep them

THE BEST SEX I EVER HAD

fresh and exciting and powerful for this moment.

I gave her an orgasm fully clothed and she was just as taken by it as ever. Then I took off her shirt and she went right ahead and took off her bra like a good girl. I proceeded with a nipple orgasm that had her once again in utter amazement.

I then got the dirty talk going dirtier and naughtier, getting her excited about going down on me. She THOUGHT it was my turn to get off, but I had other plans (hehe). She went at it and I went to town with the dirty talk and progressed into more and more suggestions about how horny my cock made her and how sucking me made her clit so hard, etc. She of course continued with her 100% success rate of feeling everything I tell her to feel and had a powerful orgasm while sucking my cock!

She knocked my wood down enthusiastically right after and then commented on how that was the wildest thing she has ever done! I want to revisit that experience, so I made the suggestion that she was going to have a lot of fun fantasizing about what just happened. She agreed, thus setting up regular rehearsal in her mind, making it a total reality for her.

Thanks man, I'm finally living my life, and you helped me make it happen.

The reason why she came so readily and often for you is because she is highly emotionally moved by you. You command respect with her. She takes what you say and do seriously. I'm not surprised she keeps coming back for more.

It is much more than "rub here, rub there." It is very much emotional and mental. You truly understand that Masterfully.

SECTION 4

GUEST CHAPTERS

Introduction from David Shade

"Although there is no metaphor that truly describes making love to a woman, the closest is playing a rare musical instrument. I wonder, does a Stradivarius violin feel the same rapture as the violinist, when he coaxes a single perfect note from its heart?"
~Don Juan DeMarco

If you have read this far... Congratulations! You now know more about women and sexuality than most men who have ever walked the face of the earth.

But I didn't write this book just to give you knowledge. I wrote this book to change lives. And that requires inspiration.

I have been inspired by various people, and I have inspired others. I wanted you to hear from some of them.

In the guest chapters that follow, you will re-discover important themes that are constant throughout this book. In each of the chapters, three by men, two by women, you will see these themes over and over again.

These aren't professional sex educators; these are people from a vast array of experiences. These are people just like you and me.

They are a hypnotist, a book publishing consultant, a former bank VP, a linguist, and a pickup artist.

What makes them unique is their clear vision into human sexuality. They say it like it is.

And two women tell you from the female perspective exactly how things are. My bet is, when you see the women saying things like:

"Women all over the world desperately long to be with a man who can unlock her sexuality." ~Lena Voyles

and

"No matter how much money a man has in the bank, a woman will lose interest if he's no good in bed." ~Alicia Dunams

You will find yourself highly motivated to put what you have learned into action. You will go out and create your life.

"How alive are you willing to be?"
~Carlos Xuma

Consider this a kick-in-the-pants to get your butt in gear. Go out and give women the incredible pleasure they so desperately desire.

Then write me and tell me your success story. Nothing would make me happier than for me to hear how great your life has become after finishing this book.

THE SECRETS OF FEMALE SEXUALITY

CHAPTER 19
MARK CUNNINGHAM

"Women are starved for screaming hot sex."
~Mark Cunningham

In the summer of 1998, I was listening to a recorded seduction seminar product. The information was somewhat interesting. But then a new speaker was introduced. He was introduced as "Major Mark, the Renegade Hypnotist". He described what he learned from thousands of hours of clinical hypnosis practice wherein most of his patients were unhappy housewives. What he shared was fascinating. This man truly understands women and their frustrations. And it was clear that he truly loved women. Never before had I heard someone with such insight and wisdom. I decided right then and there that I would someday study under this man.

I looked more into who he is. What I found is that as a teenager enlisted in the Army serving in Vietnam, his superb sharp-shooter skills were noticed and he was transferred to "the *Secret* Secret Service" and given a Major's uniform in order to carry out certain "Special Ops". Thus the name "Major" Mark.

After the war, he earned his college degree and then started a lucrative computer consulting business in California. After a few years he put away his business suit and opened a clinical practice to dedicate himself to helping people with the use of hypnosis. Interestingly, most of his clients were frustrated wealthy Valley Wives. Eventually he moved his practice to the Mid West. Along the way, he started teaching hypnosis to others and started teaching men about the reality that women live.

Because I knew that female sexuality is entirely mental, I wanted to learn the most powerful tool available; hypnosis. So in March of 2000, I attended Mark's "Stage Hypnosis" seminar. It was truly an honor to meet Mark, and it was a blast going into hypnosis and hypnotizing my fellow classmates. It was that weekend when I found my own sense of personal power.

I quickly became one of Mark's top students. I attended two more of his seminars on "Building a Better Lover". With time we became friends. Mark appeared on my "Advanced Sexual Hypnosis" program and then spoke at my Masterful Lover Super Conference in 2009.

Mark is a master hypnotist, and arguably the best in the world. He is my mentor, sensei, and guru. It is a great honor for me that he contributed a guest chapter.

Now you hear from Mark...

I was having lunch with David one recent beautiful day and, as our conversation drew to a close, he asked me if I would be willing to write something to add to his ver. 2.0 release of *Secrets of Female Sexuality*. I said yes – of course, I said yes!

I've known David for close to ten years – if you're familiar with his work at all, you've run across the story of how he came to my hypnosis seminars. I am proud and pleased to say that I taught him to see his own mistaken conditioning and how to break free of all that was holding him back and holding him down. I was there when he had the shattering insight that reality was simply what you perceived it to be. I've been cheering him on as he launched himself on a crusade to haul perfectly normal people kicking and screaming into a life filled with pleasure beyond their wildest imaginings.

But chances are that you don't know David as well as I. And given that, chances are that as you read through this book you're going to wonder just what the hell is going on! Women yearning for submission, begging for screaming hot sex, offering up their Inner Slut and generally misbehaving with all the fervor of weasels on crank? Surely, you say, there must be some exaggeration in here!

Well, no. He's not exaggerating – if anything, I'd fault him for holding back in order to shield YOUR delicate sensibilities. The plain fact of the matter is that women today are sexually starved. They feel themselves shriveling up inside for lack of passion, pleasure and satisfaction – and what's worse, they tell themselves that it's somehow their fault when they cannot find satisfaction or release in their conventional social roles. They spend their days going along to get along, and they fall asleep at night out of energy, out of time, and wondering what happened to THEIR goals. I'll wager that if you pick any modern woman at random, pump her full of infallible truth-serum and simply ask her if she is satisfied with who she's become, the nature and vehemence of her answer would curl your hair! How do I know this? Let me tell you a story…..

I'm a hypnotist. For the past 20 years I've been in the business of creating, modifying or deleting women's beliefs and behaviors. I'm actually one of the most experienced woman-whisperers in the world – I've done over 26,000 hours of sessions with women who had the great good sense to sit in my chair and offer me control. That's the bargain – they do what I tell them to do, and they get everything they've asked for in return.

And I know that right now there are men reading this who are thinking, "Sweet Jesus! 26,000 hours of women talking!" But I love women – short, tall, all ages, all backgrounds, I don't care – I can find something beautiful in any woman. And since I teach them how to lead lives free from emotional pain, to lead lives filled with passion and pleasure -- well, they tend to love me right back!

They talk to me. They pour out their heart and share their pain and loss. They cry for their lost dreams and shattered hopes. They whisper their greatest fears and, bless them all, they look at me with eyes brimming with hope that I can show them how to lead their lives better.

These women aren't broken. These women are normal. That's right, the normal well-adjusted modern woman is a jumbled-up mess inside. But she hasn't given up hope. She's smart enough to know that someone, somewhere, knows how to set her free. And she's willing to walk through fire if that's what it takes to get what she truly craves.

What I'm going to tell you here isn't just something that I made up. In fact, what I'm about to tell you is really nothing more than me channeling the thousands of women who have shared their lives with me over these two decades. You don't have to trust me on this – take these pages and show them to any and all the women in your life! Just be prepared to show that YOU understand what I'm talking about -- once expectations start to rise, you've got to live up to them. Ready?

Women are people. Wrap your mind around that thought and you're halfway home. Women are just like you, assuming that you're a person, too. They have hopes and dreams, they make foolish mistakes, they can shatter your life and/or amaze you with their selflessness. They're Good Girls, they're raving sluts, they're Moms, daughters, wives, sisters, neighbors, co-workers and friends. And they're everything on that list all wrapped up in one package. People are complex. We like to joke that the best thing about men is that we're one mood, all the time. Women are more like a major-league juggling act in front of a revolving mirror. When you stop projecting images on them, you can begin to appreciate the constantly evolving pageant that is Woman.

All women are the same. When I began my clinical practice, I was awed and challenged by the thoughts, feelings, and behaviors my clients would bring to the sessions. But after listening to the umpteenth client go on about her 'unique' problems, I began to suspect that there was a larger Truth going on. That Truth is that we are all basically the same, and we are having the same experiences. My own experience now spans sessions all around the world, and I'm telling you that women are all the same. What a fantastic opportunity this is! If you encounter something in a couple of women, chances are excellent that you'll see it again and again and again... Which means that as you learn to help, guide, affect and satisfy these women, you'll be able to do it with all the rest, as well. This is a Good Thing.

All women are different. A sex that comes up with 20 shades of green for shoes is going to put a unique and wonderful spin on everything she does. That's the beauty of it – out of a laundry list of common factors, each individual woman will create something truly her own. It's like accessorizing, only on her inside. It's up to you to bring the heart of an adventurer (and the patience of a Hero!) to the challenge of discovering just who this delightful creature has become right in front of you.

Women are who you think they are. They're not idiots – if you come up to them all full of your own preconceptions and misunderstandings, you'll get all that reflected right back at you. The easiest way to totally miss out on who a woman can truly become for you is to make stupid judgments about who she must be. In the seduction classes I've taught for men, I've heard way too many stories about men deciding who a woman is before they've ever opened their mouths. Lo and behold, that's all they ever find! This is a Bad Thing. Instead, just show up, encourage her, shut up, and let her unfold in front of you.

Women are not what you think they are. They're not delicate, frail flowers. They're not bitchy, man-eating vixens from hell. They're not vessels of Purity and Goodness. They're not an inscrutable Other – they're people with different plumbing and a way better Corpus Callosum. Befriend some and let them teach you about "women" – and then go out and test, test, test.

Now, time for some of what you're actually here for. Women crave great sex, probably more than you do. I'm serious! ALL women want to have mind-blowing, sheet-ripping sex, and they want to have lots of it, All of the time really, and they can have more of it before passing out than you can! Years ago, I started to get more playful in my clinical sessions, and so I began to throw in some attempts to shock the ladies out of their self-limiting beliefs. I tried a bunch of things, but what I finally settled on was that at some point in an early session, I'd tell them to repeat after me, "I love sucking cock!" That's right, in all my stop-smoking or weight loss or sports improvement or whatever sessions, I'd be encouraging these suburban ladies to profess a love of driving her man crazy with pleasure while sucking his cock. Much to my disappointment, this was not the shocker I had imagined. It turned out that, with the right man in the right circumstances, your average suburban sweetheart LOVED being naked, on her knees and sucking happily. And with the rare clients who had had an early bad experience, I was able to reframe their past so that without fail, in a single session they discarded their foolish imprinting and began going down with gusto. Nice to know, but not the shock induction I was looking for.

So I upped the ante. I told them all that as long as they were showing progress with their reporting problems, I'd teach them to have multiple full-body orgasms on command. Teaching them how to do it is easy – I'm a hypnotist! And again, instead of leaping out of the chair in righteous indignation, they would instead get all big-eyed and say, "You can DO that?" Not so coincidentally, my success rate with conventional therapies went sky-high! And I have very happy clients. I've had to Scotch-Guard my session chairs, but that's a small price to pay for knowledge!

Orgasms on command, multiples, prolonged orgasms, orgasms from nipple play, orgasms with anal sex, orgasms because she's sucking cock, orgasms because she's being fucked, orgasms because she's THINKING about being fucked – any and all women can learn to experience and enjoy the lot. Admittedly, I'm a hypnotist so I just put them in a profound trance and give them the experience. Build a trigger, fire it off 10 or 20 times (!) so they believe it's real, and then I give them control over it to use as they wish. Hypnosis is one shortcut. It doesn't matter that I give them complete control over it, because whoever teaches them to HAVE

THE EXPERIENCE will retain control over it, as well! This is a Very Good Thing. Plus, it makes me very popular at parties.

My peers in the therapy business are not pleased with my approach. They say that I must be acting out my own complexes, I must be being manipulative, it can't ever work and besides, women don't want this. But, do you know what? Out of thousands and thousands and thousands of women, not a single one has objected. Not one! While it is possible that I am the absolute King of mind-fuck hypnosis, there is a simpler explanation: Inside of every woman there's a horny little bitch just dying to come out and play! All I do is offer some acceptance and teach some technique, and they end up blowing their own minds.

But, you say, I'm a Master Hypnotist and so, of course, I can do this with any and all women! Yes, I am, I can and I do. But here's the genius of what David has done for you.

You can now skip my 20 year learning curve. You can skip the 26,000+ hours of listening (Yeah!) and get the knowledge reading this book. What David has done for you is to take all the risks, test all the wild-ass ideas and most importantly, gather the results together in such a way that you can sit in your chair and rapidly learn the secrets that the greatest lovers of all time spent decades uncovering.

I want you to do something very simple that will change your life for the better. I want you to read this book with the mind of a skeptic, because a skeptic doesn't just trust what they read, they instead take the information in and then test it all in their own lives. Only after they've had an experience, can they have an informed opinion.

I'm grinning as I write this, because I know what's going to happen to you. You're going to begin to find very interesting women. These women are going to desire you, because you will be able to affect them, move them, excite and satisfy them. In their intrigue, they will begin to study ways to interest, please and satisfy YOU so that they can get more of the Good Thing.

You're going to begin to stand taller, to relax more, to get playful and take some more chances. You're going to get choosy, because you're going to have way more choices. You're going to build a varied and satisfying life because sex, while plentiful and satisfying, just won't be the challenge it once was.

Rock stars are going to wish they got laid like you.

You've got to understand this – every woman wants to be understood, and you're holding the key right here, right now. EVERY woman wants to find someone who understands her like you will. And when she feels she is understood, that's when she is willing to surrender and be led. That's when she is willing to let go of who and what she was taught to be, and begin to explore all that she can be.

Frankly, you've got to learn some self-control with this. Imagine convincing a woman that you can give her richer and more satisfying pleasures than anyone she has ever known – think she's going to get attached to you? Do NOT show off your mastery of this material with women you DON'T want, because well, you'll get them, too!

Accept that you are surrounded by amazing women who are desperate for gratification and understanding. Recognize that even the most highly sought-after women are just girls inside, wanting and needing everything that all girls do. Find the open doorway that all women leave for the man who is worthy of the gift they can become, and then be man enough to take what you need and want for yourself. Recognize them for who they are, and then fuck them like you mean it.

READ THE FUCKING BOOK AND DO WHAT DAVID TELLS YOU TO DO!

Listen – David and I aren't Supermen. But we are intelligent, curious, playful, quite a bit more adventurous than the norm, and we are perfectly comfortable living outside conventional reality.

You can do these things, think these thoughts, have these feelings and get these results too. How do I know this? Because you're people, too. People can change; people can learn and grow. People like you. Yeah, that's it – people LIKE you! At least, women will – women will adore you. Men may get a bit pissed at your obvious success, but they ought to go out and buy a copy of this book themselves.

I expect great things from you all. I think David's crazy to give you all this in an inexpensive book instead of some big course offering, but that's just how he is. The least you can do is take this all in and change for the better, and when we meet out in The World, I expect to see that smile of recognition – women are actually sexy, cool creatures, and it's a Good Thing to move through the world as a Masterful Lover.

It begins now.

Mark Cunningham

davidshadelikes.com/mark

CHAPTER 20
ALICIA DUNAMS

*"There's magic in ideas, but there's reality in our actions. There's
power in our thoughts and actions in our deeds, and the only things
between our dreams and unrealized realities is ourselves."*
~Alicia Dunams

You might be curious about the thoughts of strikingly beautiful
women. Well how about if I bring you a guest chapter written by a
fashion model who strutted her stuff on the runways of Milan and
poses for numerous women's magazines? That's right, she is
smoking hot.

But what about brains? Not only does she have book smarts as a
graduate of UCLA, she has street smarts from traveling the world
solo and wrapping wealthy men around her little finger. This
woman knows what she's talking about.

But I was most interested in her experiences as a divorced
single mother, and I was most curious about her because she is a
Daddy's Girl. So I asked her to share her female point of view,
giving us the dope on what women really want.

Alicia Dunams is the author of the best-seller *"Goal Digger:
Lessons Learned from the Rich Men I Dated."* It reads like a
female version of *"Rich Dad, Poor Dad"* and *"Think and Grow
Rich"*, teaching women to believe in themselves and their own
success. She helps people learn how to make more money with her
coaching business. She teaches executives, entrepreneurs and
service-provider professionals to become household names by
writing and then leveraging their published books.

And now you hear from Alicia...

I met David Shade on a sunny day last March at a conference in Mountain View, California. He slid, quiet as a cat, into the big, stuffy room, where entrepreneurs with six-figure-plus incomes were talking about revenue growth, and sat down next to me. After an hour or so, he leaned over and whispered, "I bet you had a close relationship with your father." I've been smitten ever since.

I knew it was a compliment from the way he said it, but I didn't really understand what David meant until I got to know him better. David's theory – and it's backed up by most mental health professionals – is that women who had loving healthy relationships with their fathers make for more responsive lovers and more successful marriages because they genuinely like men. They're used to being treated well by Daddy, so they expect to have positive interactions and relationships with the opposite sex. This is one situation in which you definitely create your own reality – women who like men are liked in return.

The more I learned about David and his theories, the more I came to respect both, so when he asked me to write a guest chapter for the second edition of *"The Secrets of Female Sexuality,"* I agreed unequivocally. After all, any man whose life is dedicated to making men into better lovers is definitely my kind-a guy!

One of the unfortunate challenges facing men with regard to sexual relationships is the macho myth our culture keeps perpetuating – that *real* men are so intuitive and savvy, they just magically know what women want and can give it to them without a moment's doubt or hesitation. Not only does this put enormous pressure on men, it also turns women into little princesses who do not and should not talk; we're not supposed to tell a man what we like or he'll be insulted, since a *real* man already knows. How? I ask. This *real men* baloney is just another of those cruel myths that ends up creating a conundrum for men. It's like the old *money makes money* – how do you get money to make money *with* in the first place?

When it comes to sex, the damage done by ignorance can be devastating. After all, what is more important in an intimate relationship? Sex is the glue that holds a couple together. And what's more important to a person's self-esteem and pleasure in life than their own sexuality? Why is it such a big deal for men to admit they need to *learn* to be good lovers? Remember the old saying, "There are no stupid questions, only stupid people." Well, there are no ignorant sex questions, only ignorant lovers!

'What do women want?' has been the rallying cry for far too long. David Shade has come along to tell men exactly what women want – so that someday the question will be obsolete. In the meantime, though, while it's very much with us, every man should read this book.

I went out with and interviewed hundreds of men for my book, *"Goal Digger: Lessons Learned from the Rich Men I Dated."* While it brought me into contact with all varieties of the male gender, I can't say this experience is the one that taught me to recognize what I want from a man in bed. I knew that a long time ago: in my opinion, every woman, whether urban sophisticates on *Sex and the City* or small-town girls in Podunk, Missouri, knows deep down inside what she wants from a man in bed. Not everyone is able to verbalize it, but instinctively we know what we want when we see it – if not sooner.

Before I go any further, I must put in a word to the wise, a kind of *caveat emptor*, and that is: not every woman on the planet is the same, therefore, not every woman wants the same thing from a man. I'm speaking here primarily for myself, although I have had enough girlfriends confide in me so I know I'm fairly typical, more or less. Just don't take what I say as gospel or apply it to every single woman you meet. You have to 'suss out each female you're with, because each one is unique. Don't expect every woman to conform to everything I say.

Now then, where was I? Oh, yes: I was about to describe the kinds of qualities most women look for in a man.

There's a saying that men want a wife who'll be a lady in the living room, a workhorse in the kitchen, and a whore in the bedroom. Well, we women are not so different from men, after all: we want a husband who's a gentleman in the living room, a workhorse at the office, and an animal in bed.

Are you surprised to hear a woman use the words "animal" and "bed" together? Were you expecting to hear that I want a sweet, considerate gentleman in the bedroom? Get real! What do women want? Hell, we want to feel *wanted*! We want to know that we are so devastatingly desirable that a man can't help but ravish us, body and soul. How do we know we feel wanted? Simple – we know it when he shows it! Believe me, it's much more of a turn-on when a guy is so out-of-control with passion that his fingers fumble with the bra straps. Sure, we want you to know what's where on the female body, but heated fumbling trumps coolly skillful any day of the week.

To be explicit: if you run your hand lightly down her arm, afraid of being too rough, you're more likely to tickle than arouse her. Instead, do what comes naturally. Do what your gut, and your groin, tells you to do. Grab her arm and give it a good squeeze as you push it over her head and hold it down on the pillow to give yourself access to her breasts. And don't be tentative there, either: do what you want to do. You might want to tenderly kiss a nipple, and that's fine – but you might be dying to pull that nipple into your mouth and suck on it *hard*. If she flinches and pulls away even just a micrometer, you'll know you're being too rough, so take it down a notch. Or two. When she gets hotter later on, though, don't be afraid to kick it up a notch again and see how she reacts. The key is to pay close attention to her reactions. Far too often, men make the mistake of thinking we girls are fragile, pastel pink seashells. Give us a chance and you'll see we aren't so fragile – far from it. We like knowing someone's really *there*.

The other big mistake men make is, they don't *ask* if we like what they're doing. Yes, believe it or not, you *can* ask! I promise, she'll still respect you in the morning. The key is timing: the best time and place to ask is during sex, or later on, in afterglow. And it can be done in a really sexy way: whisper in her ear, "Do you like it hard, like *this*?" (Coordinate your movements with your words.) If she's unable to answer lucidly, it's to your credit! If she gasps and her eyes go back in her head, you're probably on the right track.

Women want men who exude confidence. By confidence, I don't mean knowing exactly what makes us hot; I mean feeling good enough about himself to know that he *will* come through in the clutch. Trust yourself. Trust that when you're both hot and sweaty, and she's climbing all over you, her sounds and moves will give you enough cues to know where to put your hands, your mouth, and other organs of pleasure. Human beings were designed for sex – if desire is built into us, can satisfaction be far behind?

Let me tell you a little secret: women hate when a guy worries about his "performance." We hate when he thinks of lovemaking as a *performance*, good or bad. If we want a performance, we'll go to the opera! In bed, we want spontaneity, reality, blood-and-guts honesty. So, drop the "performance" – unless you're in a play.

We don't expect sex with Superman. We know "it takes two to tango," and that whatever happens between us in bed happens *between us*. When we make love, neither one of us is doing it alone. We're doing it together, so how 'good' or 'bad' it is depends on chemistry and interactions between two of us. If a man is relaxed and lets his feelings flow, sex will flow, too.

We want men to be generous in bed. No woman wants a man who's in it for his pleasure alone—a man who takes and takes and takes. We want a man to have our best interests at heart, and to know that the way to get us to give up the goods is by first giving. That obviously means giving us sexual pleasure – but it also means giving of yourself outside the bedroom. If a man spends the first half of the evening talking nonstop about himself, bragging about his accomplishments, never asking us anything, then we already know he's not a giving soul, and he won't change when he gets into bed. We'll never find out for sure: this guy isn't going to get in our bed. Ever.

Generosity is complicated. It's not only about money, but money is part of it. The truth is, no matter how much money a man has in the bank, a woman will lose interest if he's no good in bed. And yet, as I've just said, one aspect of being "good in bed" is being generous – and before they even get to the bedroom, a woman usually knows if a man is or is not generous. Does he open the car door for her, or just sit there playing with the radio dial while she climbs in? Does he pay the check with little fanfare, or does he make a big show of it? Does he leave a decent tip? Worst of all, does he divvy up the check, expecting her to pay half? That sets off alarm bells in every woman's head. A proclivity to financial stinginess signals a reluctance to give in other areas, period.

I know a woman who served her stunned husband with divorce papers the minute the last kid went off to college. She had been waiting for this moment for 25 years—a quarter century, during which he never let her redecorate the house, made her feel guilty when she bought herself anything, and wouldn't allow her to hire a cleaning person. This man was a billionaire—a cheap billionaire. Men who are cheap with money are usually cheap with their emotions, their touches, and their kisses. Money does talk, after all, and when it says *you can't have me*, any woman with half a brain runs the other way.

In bed, generosity is as simple as sometimes giving pleasure without getting any yourself – temporarily, that is. If you're pleasing her orally and she's just lying back enjoying it without doing anything to you in return, don't take it the wrong way. When a woman gets like this, she isn't being passive or selfish. What's happened is she's reached a place where she trusts you and has fully surrendered to the sensations you're giving her. Every woman wants to be in this place, so if you can take her there, baby, you're in. Literally. (I'm being explicit again here.) She may not be pleasuring you in that moment, but I guarantee your turn will come. The key is to stop wondering when your turn will come, which you do by learning to genuinely enjoy giving pleasure. It's very powerful to see a woman in that open, vulnerable state, and realize *you* made her that way. Awesome!

To recap, here are my five minimum requirements of how to be 'good in bed':

Learn. Learn *in general* what women want by reading, talking to other men, and using David's wonderful products. Learn what a specific woman wants by paying close attention and following her cues.

Let it rip. Unleash your animal sexuality. Don't worry about being 'polite' – there's a time and a place for everything. Remember: a gentleman in the living room, a workhorse at the office, and an animal in bed.

Be confident. You are a sexual being with a right to good sex, and you will know how to please a woman as long as you're relaxed and fully present with her.

Don't perform. Be yourself!

Be generous. Be generous of heart. Give of yourself emotionally. Give with your body. Give pleasure, in bed and everywhere else. In the living room, be a gentleman by not dominating the conversation; instead, encourage her to talk, and listen attentively. In the bedroom, listen to what her body is telling you and follow her cues. Cultivate the ability to get pleasure from giving pleasure.

If you practice these five basic principles, I promise, you will never again have to worry about being 'good in bed.' You will be.

Alicia Dunams

davidshadelikes.com/alicia

CHAPTER 21
CARLOS XUMA

"A man must DO or he never truly lives his life."
~Carlos Xuma

I had heard a lot of good things about this independent seduction instructor by the name of Carlos Xuma. I had admired his writings and his products. It all hit upon the heart of the matter, and that is to be a man. It is certainly a topic I cover with my clients.

I had the honor of meeting Carlos in May of 2007 at a dinner in San Francisco to bring together local experts before my talk the next day. Carlos was a very genuine man. He used to be a guitar player in a rock band and then moved to teaching Karate. He stands apart from most seduction gurus in that he teaches men to get in touch with their masculinity and their purpose as a man.

Carlos and I quickly became friends and collaborated on telling our respective clients about each other. It was an honor for me to have Carlos speak at my Masterful Lover Super Conference in Vegas in 2009, and it is an honor for me that he has contributed a chapter here.

And now you hear from Carlos...

ALPHA MALE (MAN) SEXUALITY

Let's be clear: David Shade has helped men everywhere re-establish their sexuality with women by showing them the true nature of women in the bedroom.

Hell, I still remember reading my raw, dog-eared copy of "*The David Shade Manual*" so many "wild, screaming orgasms" ago.

Now, what you're about to read may push you to the point of feeling completely liberated from your fears of women and giving them what they really want...

Or it just might piss you off completely.

Either way, strap yourself in. It's going to be a bumpy ride that I hope you'll never forget.

You see, I'm the emotional bully that wants to shove you enough times so that you finally snap out of it and get pissed enough to shove back. Because I really don't need you as my friend. In fact, I'd be happy if I knew you hated me so much that you got up and got motivated to do something with your life just to spite me.

I'm the mean, nasty voice of your dad that knows that in order to make a man of you, I have to risk you not liking me. That's the price I pay to make a boy be all he can be, to win his own life back and become a man of passionate excellence that women would sacrifice everything to have. Sure, I'm a cool guy in real life. I'm just more concerned about getting you out of your rut and into ACTION with women.

Many years ago, I gave up any pretense of trying to win over people and make everyone "like" me, or even to make some kind of powerful "statement." If I'm trying to be profound, I'm probably not being very authentic, because then my misdirected goal is to make me sound like a brilliant guy, instead of getting the job done for YOU.

If David had waited for approval from someone to release his fantastic programs on exploring sexuality and REALLY pleasing a woman (not just wham-bam-thankyouma'am) we'd never have heard of him...

Being approved of is the sure path to misery and doom on this planet. And so in this brief time I have with you, I intend to leave you fired up and full of "piss and vinegar," as the old timers say. You'll either hate me forever - or you'll find a nugget of something here that kicks your ass hard enough to make you want to make a real change.

Either way, you need to feel SOMETHING. And hopefully, DO *something*.

The real tragedy in life is to have avoided offending someone, and, therefore, avoided pleasing anyone to the degree you could have.

Have you ever suspected you were put here to accomplish great things?

And mixed in with that suspicion is another deeper pain of thinking you may never accomplish them? Not because you aren't really capable of doing them - you're just afraid that you won't be able to get out of your own way long enough to actually do them.

For many years now, I've been associated with this term of "Alpha Male" and my more specific model of the "Alpha Man." I've taken a lot of pride in helping thousands of guys elevate themselves from their more passive lifestyles into one of powerful success with women (and in all parts of their lives).

But what does it really mean to be the "Alpha" today?

AND, just as importantly, how does being an Alpha Man benefit you in getting the kind of success you imagine with women?

First of all, here is what an Alpha Man is NOT:

He is NOT the "aggressive" jerk out there, pushing people around to prove his dominance.

A true "Alpha" understands his role also requires compassion. Being an Alpha Man means reaching the apex of the pyramid of his own development.

He's not a bully. He's not a brute.

He's got the amount of interpersonal finesse that allows him to move through any social situation with the cool, fluid motion of a Manta Ray.

He is never stingy—with praise, love, help, drive, excitement, passion...

The list can go on and on, but what I'm driving at here is that a man with a powerful grip on his own energy is a source, a wellspring of energy to those around him.

Think of the energy that a woman releases in orgasm, the mounting obliteration of logical thought into a raving, writhing concubine of lust. Energy is meant to be released in the world, not stored up in batteries, because when your masculine energy is constipated, you lose with women.

He is not in "defense mode."

In other words, a true Alpha Man has resolved his petty childhood traumas and has moved on in his life.

If it sounds insensitive to call your childhood issues "petty," let me remind you that they do not exist anywhere in the universe but in your head. And they are quite probably your biggest roadblock to getting where you want to go. If you identify with those issues and past "limitations," let me remind you that I'm friends with a man who is 3 feet tall, will never walk, could break a rib just sneezing, and is more of an inspiration than most "normal" people I know. (Thank you, Sean.)

Get over yourself.

Your whiney stories of self-entrapment in your past don't mean SHIT to me or anyone else, so just do us all a favor and save them for your "cry in the pillow" night.

"You're put here to *create* yourself,
not to discover yourself."
~Unknown

It's time to shut down that old radio station that you tune into every convenient moment when you need an excuse to protect your self-image or your identity. Listening to that station will give you a bad case of "PITY ME - because that's the only sick, twisted way I can feel good about myself."

Yeah, I know there's a lot of self-serving therapists that would love to indulge you and let you wallow in the "cannot be changed" past. But you can't afford to fall into that trap. All great men have let go of the past enough to get on with their lives.

Okay, I'm done being intentionally abrasive.

Mostly.

Now, let's talk about...

What an Alpha Man IS:

Motivated

This is probably the one trait that guys would never suspect is at the heart of all the men I know who are successful with women. And I'm not referring to the motivation to get better with women—even if that is an important element. The motivation I'm talking about here is the ability to tap into your most valuable and precious form of ENERGY.

This is the ability to find the REASON—the Why that makes you do something you know you need to do.

It's the thing you can't get out of your head, no matter how much you try.

Back around 2001, I was a Vice President at a well-known investment bank. I had the money, the car, the clothes, and so on.

I was walking back to my office building in the financial district of San Francisco, blowing on my Starbucks coffee as I made my way toward the building, when I saw an image stenciled on the sidewalk. Seven words were written underneath, and I found myself stopped in my tracks, steaming java in hand, and staring at the cement like a confused dog.

It said: "How alive are you willing to be?"

Wow.

That phrase would repeat itself in my head many times when I was taking care of my ailing mother. When she passed away, I got around to finally answering the question for myself.

Because I wasn't living a life - I was making a living.

I got haunted by those seven words, and they still kick my ass every time I look at a decision. Do I do this to be "safe," or do I do this to LIVE a little more?

Let me equate it for you in simple terms: Women want a man who is connected to his passion and motivation for life.

And if I phrase it in the opposite - the negative way - you'll probably understand it much more clearly:

Women DON'T WANT a man who is dead, unmotivated, and disconnected from his reason for living.

Women need men (more than ever) who know why they're here—both in the small picture of taking the lead in the bedroom, and in the big picture of carving their own path in life.

It's been said that there are two big questions in life: Where am I going? and Who will come with me?

If you get those questions in the wrong order, you're in BIG trouble.

Taking the leadership role in the bedroom is an absolute must if you're going to fulfill a woman sexually. It's the cornerstone of David Shade's teachings, and one of the critical lessons I expanded into a life philosophy.

An Alpha Man is exceptionally skilled at managing his energies.

There are six primary forms of energy a man has in his life, and he has to budget and channel this power effectively if he's ever going to achieve the great goals he is capable of.

- Sexual Energy
- Psychological Energy
- Emotional Energy
- Physical Energy
- Spiritual Energy
- Social Energy

Guess which one has the most power?

Yup, you got it...Sexual. Think of all the things men have done/created/destroyed/re-created throughout history just to cut a Grade-A prime slice of Goddess. It's been said that all of man's achievements have been to find a constructive outlet for sexual energy.

That's why you must, must, MUST manage your sexual energy as a man. Don't waste it on mindless porn sessions, or cheating, or solo flights of monkey-spanking fancy. Instead, channel that energy into the creative force that it is. Don't cheat yourself of the ability to leverage that sexual potency.

I remember laying in bed next to many a fine young lady, post-orgasm cuddling, and thinking, "Wow, that was what I was in such a hurry to get to...?" Five or ten seconds of release. That's it. And all the effort before and during sex seems almost silly when you're all done. Why not take some time to make something of the mounting pleasure? Re-direct your vital life force - explore and enjoy the build-up of tension instead of running for the finish line. You'll start really appreciating the saying, "The point is not the destination; it's the journey."

An Alpha Man is POLARIZED.

This is the way we express our masculinity to women, and it's the one part of a man's overall sexual energy that is so completely lacking in our modern world.

Consider how women are attracted to Men. Yes, even most gay and lesbian couples you've met have a male/female dynamic to them. There has to be a polarity of energy or there's nothing to be attracted to.

Have you ever tried to force yourself to feel attraction for a woman when there was no chemistry there? Didn't work so well, did it? Well, it doesn't work for women, either, especially when the guy is working harder to convince her logically rather than create emotional attraction.

You need the Yin-Yang.

You need the positive-negative.

You need these polarities to keep your sexual attraction alive over the long-term, or you'll wind up more like brother and sister than man and woman.

He 'OWNS' every encounter with a woman.

Most men are emotionally and sexually constipated.

They are holding back from FEELING their own lives. They avoid those feelings of depression and pain, but at the cost of their own joy and passionate fire.

After having coached guys from many different countries, one thing stands out as the common denominator for guys who have problems attracting women. They're just unable to let themselves go.

Their personality is restrained. Their vibrancy is chained. Their enthusiasm is feigned.

You could do away with 90% of the seduction and attraction techniques by simply removing the shackles that keep your personality shut off and muted.

You might be reading this and thinking, "Wow, that would mean I'd have to change." In fact, you're not really even thinking it. Just a small part of your inner reluctance peeked out like a groundhog from its hole and made you scared for a second. That reluctance is your mind's natural defense mechanism. The problem is that it's stopping you from being all that you can be.

Most people think change takes time.

It doesn't.

Most REAL change happens in an instant. Like a man whose lung x-rays with an ominous shadow inspire him to throw his cigarettes in the garbage.

Or a man who sees his newborn boy for the first time, goes home, and empties his bottles of bourbon and beer down the drain.

Or the guy who gets pushed around once too many, and joins a gym and a dojo.

Real change happens in an instant, or not at all. If you can put it off, you're not ready to change because there's no reason to make it happen. Without that force - that REASON - you'll just keep finding clever excuse after clever excuse for why you don't have to change.

If it can happen later, it will probably never happen.

No rush... It's just your life you're pissing away.

Change is a bolt of lightning, a sudden transition from what was to what is. It's NOW. It's a desire that screams out for immediate redemption.

The only kind of change that takes time is the kind that you ALLOW to happen in your life, and it's usually the Bad Kind.

- Days wear on, and you manage to avoid calling that girl back because you were afraid of running out of conversation...

- Months roll by, and you let yourself eat junk and live vicariously through the lives of people on television to numb your aching soul. Now, you're fat and sickly...

- Years pass, and you've forgotten what that feeling was to love your girlfriend, or your wife, so now you're dead and floating downstream.

- Decades go by, and maybe now you're a pessimist that can't let go of his own negativity and frustration...

Slow change is the kind that turns you into a cautionary tale - rehearsed victim behavior and bitter resentment.

Slow change will kill you, my brother.

Hey, it's always convenient to find a reason to look away from the pain and the struggle and think, "It's okay. It's not THAT BAD." But I urge you to re-evaluate your threshold of acceptance. Don't be numbed into an average life.

Think of it this way: What else have you got to do with your life but become the best you can be? One day, your days here will be done, and you can relax in your pine box or your urn on the mantle. The only stress-free existence is for the man who's laid out horizontal and his eyes have been closed forever.

You're going to be on your path of growth, of living a REAL Alpha Man's life, when you stop turning your eyes away from the parts of your life that make you uncomfortable.

"Ooh, that was unpleasant. Better not do that again."

Hell NO!

The goodies in this world go to the man that barrels right through ten miles of "ouch" to get to the soft juicy center of his dreams.

The next time you find yourself shying away or quitting, just tell yourself that anything less than facing it and overcoming it is being a douche-bag PUSSY, and you don't deserve the balls you were born with.

In fact, just hand over your nut-sack to someone who might be able to do something with them.

Are you getting mad yet? A little steamed? Hot under the collar?

Here's the Truth: We're all self-made...

But only the successful admit it.

Be the hero in your life. Instead of some foul-mouthed rapper or drug-addicted athlete, why can't YOU be your kids' hero?

That's the way it oughta be.

Let me be perfectly clear with you on this one point, so that I'm not mistaken for some new-age, "politically correct," touchy-feely chump:

If you don't find a purpose and go after it in this life, YOU'RE NOT A MAN.

It's our birthright and our legacy. Women have their own power in their nurturing strength, but you must seek challenges and overcome them. It's who we are.

A man must DO or he never truly lives his life. He dies unfulfilled and wistful.

In the great book "*The Alchemist*" by Paulo Coelho, the boy, Santiago, is kicked out on his ass by his true love, Fatima. She refuses to have anything to do with him until Santiago goes after his "Personal Legend," his passion in life. Fatima tells him that if he settles now and never goes after his calling, he'll lose the fire that makes him a man; his eyes will always carry a glimmer of what "might have been." She knows how pathetic it is for a man to not chase his own legend - and how miserable it would be for her to live with him.

I'm passing on this one call to action to you:

Get pissed off.

The sad fact is that we don't change unless we're pushed to our limits, angered and disgusted with the situation we're in. The secret of motivation is to get yourself to that limit as fast as you possibly can.

Because while you wait for it to happen on its own, you're dying. One day at a time, you're creeping slowly toward the finish line.

To be a man is to cross that line and know that you did what had to be done, and you're proud of the race you ran.

Carlos Xuma

Strength & Honor

davidshadelikes.com/carlos

CHAPTER 22

LENA VOYLES

"The most critical factor for good sex is that the man lead.
In our post-feminist society, we (women or men) are not very well
conditioned to be prepared for the inevitability of that reality."
~Lena Voyles

Gathered within my VIP Inner Circle are some of the world's greatest lovers. These are enlightened educated men who love giving women incredible pleasure. They are the Masterful Lovers. There are also a number of women who join in order to communicate in a place that is safe and accepting. Discussions of all matters take place, without judgment or condemnation. The wealth of advanced level knowledge is stand-alone.

Of all the women who joined, one is especially impressive. Lena Voyles truly understands the philosophy of Masterful Lover, and can clearly articulate the feminine perspective.

When Lena first joined the VIP Inner Circle Online Forum, she posted this introduction:

> Most of you are here to uncover the inner workings of the female mind. I'm here to snoop through the inner workings of the male mind. And you thought women were challenging to work out.
>
> I also hope I can provide some perspective from the point of view of an attractive, educated 23 year old woman-you know, just in case you're interested ;)

I am completely fascinated by NLP as my M.A. is in Linguistics. We never touched on it in school and that amazes me because it reveals so much about how the brain processes language.

I am convinced that sex as it should be is one of the highest spiritual experiences a person can have. I'm sure some of you will agree with me and some of you will disagree, but I'd love to have some chats with those who do agree and aren't afraid of the esoteric.

My biggest dating challenge has probably always been finding someone who is intelligent enough to be quicker than I am and remain the dominant party. Hanging around here reminds me that there are some truly awesome guys in the world, and it is an instant pick-me-up :D

If you want an opinion, just ask. I've read all of David's books. And yes, David really is right. Really.

To give you a further example of her insight, I shall refer to one particular discussion in the VIP Inner Circle Online Forum, where a member asked a question about his leading in the bedroom being challenged. I responded by writing, "A DOM never validates challenges." Lena replied to the member's question with the following:

In my experience this is where so many guys get stuck. Even pretty confident, attractive, high self esteem guys. And it is almost guaranteed that once a woman takes an interest in you, you are going to get challenged at some point, probably at some sort of critical emotional junction (whether you realize the underlying emotional significance of the moment or not). We won't

THE SECRETS OF FEMALE SEXUALITY

bother to mess with your head unless we're really interested in you (so, as David says in his writings, take it as a GOOD sign – she seems to be sending out these negative vibes, but she's actually saying, 'this matters to me, this matters to me, this matters to me – I am emotionally invested now').

Men who wouldn't bat an eye at a challenge from another man can get suckered in when challenged by a woman that they care about. Of course, one approach is to not care about anyone. These are the Bad Boys – we know all about them. I don't even have to go there.

But the good guys are all too often tempted to respond as if it were a normal rational conversation. Well, um, it's NOT a normal rational conversation. We're not actually asking a question in search of the right answer. We're looking to see that 'who you are' remains consistent no matter how weird your surrounding environment gets. And we want to know that your feelings for us are strong enough not to be altered by our 'moods'.

I think that being a Dom very simply boils down to: Love me as I really am or leave (no in between), and You have no control over what I feel for you (this is different from giving her the power to make you happy or sad, e.g. "It makes me so happy when you are so responsive to me..."). She needs to know that she can please you while you are beyond her control. I am firmly of the opinion that this is actually a really, really natural state for most men.

So it was an obvious choice for me to ask Lena to share her thoughts on Female Sexuality.

246   www.DavidShade.com

And now you hear from Lena...

The essence of female sexuality is "Surrender". And for a woman to surrender completely, to place her fate in the hands of her lover, there must be a certain degree of security, a sense of commitedness. This security, however, does NOT take the form of spoken promises so much as it takes form in her knowing that she completely satisfies *him* – that she makes her man wildly happy, and that she has the potential to fulfill his every fantasy. This is what women *live* for – believe it or not. So believe it! A woman longs to feel cherished, adored, and to know that she is always Number 1 in her man's heart, and she also *knows* that this is only possible if being with her brings him the sex life of his dreams. A woman is always in the often uncomfortable position of longing for her man to be completely fulfilled, and yet knowing that his fulfillment depends totally on his own initiative. For it goes against the fundamental grain of her being to 'drive' the action. She can respond, admire, adore, praise, fawn, and surrender. But she cannot Create. The power of Creation, of choosing what the relationship will be and what road it will travel, is yours as a man. And all that you can look for in a woman is an eagerness to follow that lead – albeit an eagerness that, under the right lead, will blossom and snowball into what seems like a force of its own!

A woman needs to experience everything that makes her man a Man – from his penchant for bungee jumping to his financial ambitions to his sexual intensity – *even though she may not enjoy acting that way herself.* To illustrate: men enjoy seeing women in makeup and push-up bras – obviously, men do not enjoy wearing makeup and push-up bras themselves! What men actually enjoy is seeing women express their feminine nature. The converse is true of women. Further, men must express their nature fully, strongly, confidently. Masterful Lover is, at its core, the mind sets that give birth to that expression. In many respects, David's works are the key to one's own innate manhood. And women the world over desperately long to be with a man who can unlock that and show them everything that is inside. And I do mean EVERYTHING.

A high self esteem woman is open to sexual advances 24/7, provided one thing is true: she does not feel pressured. Attentiveness has got to be one of the very most intoxicating qualities in a man. And attentiveness does NOT mean trying to do what you think she wants you to do – it does not mean doing all those things that come under the heading of "thoughtfulness" – no, it means reading how she is feeling in the moment. Pushing everything else out of your mind and simply paying attention to what she is telling you about herself right now. A high self esteem woman *always* wants as much sexual attention as she can comfortably handle. Even if she decides for other reasons that she does not want to pursue a relationship with you, she will take your appreciation of her as a compliment – she will not be offended. Also, there will be times when 'as much as she can handle' is simply you holding her hand protectively – do not underestimate the power of such moments. A man's protective behavior is always very sexualized in the mind of a woman. This has been the root of many an office romance: a man has brotherly protective feelings for a co-worker and the woman in question responds sexually. Genuine, masculine protectiveness always plants seeds of eroticism in the back of a woman's mind. In a relationship with a high self esteem woman, never, never pretend to feel indifferent toward her – it will smash her ego for sure, and very probably piss her off (and rightly so!) Perhaps it's a little cruel, but we want the intensity of male desire in our lives at all times, whether we are in a position to respond or not. Sex is so very, very much a mental game for us – we are building up to 'the moment' in our minds days, (sometimes even weeks or months!) before so much as touching our partner.

Because of this, we adore mind games. We want to flirt with you from the moment we wake up in the morning, however subtly. Yes, there are lots of social environments in which that flirting might be more geeky or humorous than sexual, but we still crave the connection and the deeply sexual vibe that underlies it.

Choose a woman with a strong sense of imagination, and I guarantee it will be easier to lead her mentally than you think! The imagination is an essentially limitless world, and a man's power in a woman's imagination is limited only by his own imaginings. (Hint, hint: this is why it is so important to accept and be in touch with your own fantasies). If you get her mind stirred up before approaching her body, you are guaranteed pretty much any success you choose. Make her imagine something vividly first, have her day-dreaming of it, have *her* wondering in anticipation, and when push finally comes to shove you can be guaranteed that she will love the experience and that she will love what you have done to her. By playing a woman's mind, you can take something that otherwise she might describe as "enjoyable" and make her ache with longing for it. Downright torture her with anticipation! We dream of being commanded in this way. In order to get inside her mind, pay attention to her own fantasies. It is ridiculously easy to get a (high self esteem) woman to tell you her fantasies. We have been all pent up with them boiling inside of us for years. We will jump at the opportunity to let them out – very little stealth is required; David tells you more than you need to know. It almost embarrasses me to reveal just how easy we are when it comes to this!

Never, ever mistake shyness or primness for disinterest. Women are innately aware of the power of sex. We are aware that some people would make very dangerous 'partners' indeed. And we have an innate sense of the "hair-trigger" quality that male sexuality can have. We don't want to set anyone off accidentally. We don't want to be "sexual bullies". And we don't want to find that we've led on the wrong person, say, "oops, my mistake", and back-pedal our way out of a situation of our own making. So we wait for a man to take the lead and the responsibility. Shyness is often a kind of respect for the enormity of sex. And underneath that shyness can be such eagerness for exploration and adventure; such an eagerness to be led.

Once your own hang-ups and misconceptions fade into the distance, a woman becomes a road map to her own fulfillment, and yours – all you have to do is read the signals that she constantly gives off. Respond naturally, confidently. You have the correct beliefs and the tools in your toolkit to go the distance. And once her expectations have been exceeded, then you chart by your own stars. A woman needs a self-fulfilled man – a man who walks the walk in all areas of his life, whom she can respect and admire first from afar. And once he has led her to know herself in a way she could never have done without him opening her up, then she needs to experience everything that is "Other" – everything that makes him male, innately different to her, the other half of the species, the other side of this two-part puzzle. Lead your woman to know you – you exactly as you really are without fear. Make it safe and exciting. Start on her terms and change them into yours. Make her feel secure by showing her how much she excites you. Thrill her with the edginess of passion and the unexpected. String her along and string her along and string her along with constant mind play, until you are both living the life of your dreams.

Begin by learning the truth, and continue by seeking it always.

"There are more things in heaven and earth, Horatio, than are dreamt of in your philosophy"
~Hamlet, scene V

Lena Voyles

CHAPTER 23
BRAD P

"Women can't help themselves with Bad-Boys!"
~Brad P.

I spoke at a conference in Montreal in the summer of 2006. My speech was about sexuality. The other speakers were to speak about pick-up. There was word that a new fast rising super-star was scheduled to speak, a guy named Brad P. However, nobody knew what he looked like.

During the breaks, people would gather outside to enjoy the weather and some conversation. A tall lanky guy walked up to me. He was wearing skin tight black jeans, a black T-shirt, Keds tennis shoes, and long straggly hair. He reminded me of Joey Ramone. He said, "Hi David, I'm Brad P. I have your Manual, and I love it!" He started telling me about all the things he had done with women, such as instant orgasm on command, extended orgasms, squirting orgasms, threesomes; you name it, he had done all the things he learned in my Manual. While we were talking, it became apparent to me that this guy truly had it. Not only was he a giant among pick-up artists, he is one of the rare ones who actually loves everything to do with "service after the sale." And he is really good.

We quickly became friends and started doing business together. Brad interviewed me for his 30/30 Club membership. I invited Brad to speak at my 2009 Masterful Lover Super Conference in Vegas. He was a huge hit. So it was an obvious choice for me to ask him to write a guest chapter here.

Now you hear from Brad...

David Shade once told me that women exist in a constant state of tension between wanting to be a good girl and wanting to be slutty. I've found that this is true for every woman I've ever met, but what differs from one woman to the next is how they express this tension and how they justify this tension.

It's a matter of personal style. It's a matter of her social and cultural background. It's depends on where she's at in life.

During the process of sexual escalation, it's normal for a woman to resist several times, and it is normal for a man to be persistent, patiently trying over and over until she finally becomes sexually submissive.

Many men perceive this process of resistance and persistence as nothing more than an annoying roadblock on the way to sex. However, it can serve several important functions. It's a way of getting to know each other. It's a way to get the other person to show their true colors. And, most importantly, it makes the sex that comes later more intense. Resistance and persistence is the flame that makes sex so hot.

Let me tell you a little story about the greatest sex I've ever had in my life. Keep in mind that I've had sex with quite a large number of women. I've been working as a professional pickup artist for the last five years, and having a large number of sexual partners is part of the job. But this one was different. I've never seen anything like it before, and I haven't seen anything like it since. She will go down in the record books as the best ever.

We first met in San Diego when I was 28 years old. She was 19 at the time. I was playing my guitar with a few friends, and she approached me after I finished up. "Hey, good playing, Craig," she said. "Thanks, but it's Brad," I responded. "Oh, someone told me your name was Craig."

I didn't find myself terribly attracted to her at first. She looked a little rough around the edges. She was a hippy chick. Her shirt didn't fit right, she looked a bit messy, but there was just something about her.

As I talked to her for a few more minutes, I picked up on a few things that made this girl very unusual. First, there was something going on with her body. Something looked out of proportion, but I couldn't tell what because her clothes were so strange. I would come to find out later that this girl had been blessed with a pair of natural double D breasts and an extreme hourglass figure. Her large breasts hung a bit too far forward over a small waist which curved out at drastic angles into a pair of nice wide hips. It was like something out of a cartoon or an animated film, but at her age, she had little awareness of how attractive and powerful this was.

The other thing I picked up on was her sexual energy. She was direct and free flowing. She would touch people right away without even thinking anything of it. She touched me fairly quickly, and I knew something about her was different and special.

Let me pause for a moment and mention that I like boobs. A lot. Boobs like that are hard to come by, that's for sure. I took her to the beach at night with her cock blocking friend and my drunken wing, and I couldn't get anywhere. She's religious and a virgin at age 20. But she stayed in touch and showed a lot of interest, so I saw her again when I went to San Jose about a year later.

This time it was a totally different story. We were driving around and decided to go to the water park right before it was closing. When we got to the gate, we saw a man and a woman get turned away since it was closing time. So what did we do? We walked right past the ticket takers, ignored them, and got in free.

We snuck around the place making out and she ended up jerking me off in the public restroom. I spread her gorgeous body naked on the concrete behind a tree and ate her pussy. We had been sneaking around the place for a while, and the park was closed by that point. I could tell that the danger of being in the park when it was closed was exciting for this repressed Christian girl.

We eventually got caught by the guy who cleans the bathrooms and had to make a break for it. We climbed a fence and got the hell out of that place before they could call the cops on us. This hot

Spanish chick who managed the park scolded us on the way out, "We don't do that here." Hahaha, well we do. Hehe.

So, we ended up going back to the place I was staying at, and she wrapped those huge titties around my cock and gave me the tit fucking of my life! I usually avoid virgins at all costs, but this time it was worth it.

Fast forward about another year. She was living in NY for a few months, and I was there, too. So, we get in touch, we hang out and I bring her to my place. This whole interaction became a battle of wills, a test of my persistence, and a test of skill. I fuck those huge tits again. And this time she blows me, too, but I couldn't get her to take out the pussy. No matter. This girl blew me and took a big load on the face. It was about 30 minutes of head and tit fucking. Sweet! It's almost better than normal, cause I fuck girls all the time, but rarely do I tit fuck a set like that.

This is where the persistence comes in and things really start getting heated up. I was trying over and over to touch her pussy, but she would stop me every time. After she stopped me, I'd always wait five or ten minutes, then I'd get her horny and try again. Over and over we repeated this cycle.

I never got slowed down by this small rejection. At this point, I was thinking she did want me to touch her, but she has all kinds of issues about it, so, in a way, it just makes it hotter cause it's a battle in her mind.

Sexual arousal vs. sexual repression. It was the classic good girl/ bad girl conflict that David Shade always talks about. Every woman has it, but in this case it was more intense because she had an extremely high libido and also deeply held religious beliefs.

After the ninth time being persistent, she let me get my fingers in. That was the next morning. The last straw was when I put her on her belly and pulled her hair, biting her neck. That maneuver is so dominating that the girl just wanted to submit as much as possible. She refused to come. This girl puts a moral dilemma on anything that results in pleasure. So, she will only come in a relationship, as I found out later. In the next meet up, I will use that to my advantage further.

The following week, she calls me to get together. She and a friend are coming to my part of town for a haircut appointment. Now ya know I don't wanna deal with the friend. So, I tell her I'm busy. Why take a step back? I'm advancing so nicely with this girl.

A few days later, she invites me out to her place because her roommate is going to be away. That sounds better to me, so I agree. I get there and we hang out for a bit. She cooks dinner. We watch TV. One of my boys drops off the DVDs of my seminar, and she is begging me to see it. I tried to avoid it, but I didn't want to seem like I had something to hide so I put on the part about how to act on a date, where to take a girl, etc. That stuff is not as hardcore as other parts of my seminar, so this works well. It leads to a discussion about her trip to England. It turns out this girl went on a sugar-daddy dating auction. A bunch of rich guys in their 50s show up and bid for dates with hot young women. She said she really wanted to have a rich guy to take her to theater events, but she just couldn't get attracted to them so she never returned their emails.

Typical stuff. Girl tries to logically convince herself to be attracted and cannot do it. She's talking about how she knows bad boys like me are a terrible idea, but she just can't help herself. I'm going along with it all. I tell her to be careful of guys like me.

Into the bedroom to get down to business. More of the same: a battle of wills. This time I know even better what will work with her. But she knows even better how to resist. The game is even harder now. This girl is smart and thoroughly indoctrinated by the church.

I end up getting her all hot, then when I try for some oral, she's got a comeback ready: "Only with someone who loves me." So, I go into freeze out mode. I lie next to her and don't touch her. She says she's been thinking about it for a while and she just wants to be friends. Now keep in mind we're both naked and horny. She caught me off guard with that one, but I always handle that the same. "I was just about to ask you the same thing," I tell her.

It's always a good idea to mirror what the girl is doing when she tries to take a step back. This keeps you from looking needy. This is true in cold approach, when a girl turns her back on you, you turn yours, too. It's also true in relationships, which is the case with this girl. Anytime you hear "Let's just be friends" or "We're not having sex tonight" or anything where the girl is trying to draw the line or shut your down using words, a great response is, "I was just about to tell you the same thing."

Now, the whole interaction becomes largely intellectual. I tell her, "I was thinking we should just be friends cause I don't think you're gonna be able to handle this, etc."

Her point is: "I've been thinking that for a while, I just keep putting it off and saying one more time, and then we'll be friends." She talks about past relationships and how she has never had a happy one because she moves around for college all the time. She keeps saying, "I feel like a whore." I ask "In a good way or in a bad way?" She says in a bad way. So, I'm done with her for now, and she needs a good talking to.

I tell her she's got issues and that's why I had the feeling we shouldn't be involved. Her first issue is that she has a narrow-minded view of relationships.

There are many forms of success in relationships. If you think that the only successful relationship is one that leads to marriage, then you are shutting yourself out to a great deal of happiness and setting yourself up for disappointments in life.

The second issue is that she lives in the future or the past but does not experience the present in a whole-hearted way. She thinks every relationship is going to be lousy like her past relationships. That's living in the past. She is so scared of getting her heart broken that she refuses to open up to someone. That's living in the future.

The third issue I bring up is that she has an unrealistic ideal relationship in her head, and comparing that to relationships in the real world is a source of pain and disappointment for her.

I tell her all of this in a patient, caring way, of course, but the frame is that since she does not have her shit together, she is not good enough for me. I can be a pretty compelling speaker; my philosophy degree was coming in handy for this one. She was impressed at the depth of my knowledge and is still attracted to me.

Then we move on to some sex talk. I tell her, "I know that you have all these issues, but at the same time you are a highly charged, sexual kind of person. You probably think about me all the time and the way I make you extremely horny. You feel so dirty but you love it. That's why when I pull your hair and hold you down, you can't resist it. You know you'd never be able to take my big cock in your pussy but you still like to think about it sometimes." She's agreeing with everything. So, I keep going. "The fact that you know you're doing something so wrong just makes this hotter for both of us. You can't stop yourself, and that's an amazing feeling." She says how she loves the fact that I'm so rough with her.

Now, of course, the girl is raging horny, so I'm gonna take this opportunity to drop a load before it's too late. I lay her on her belly again and start roughing her up. Biting, pulling hair, pushing her around. She loves it. She's saying "yes! more!" So, I flip her over and put my dick back between those huge tits. I fuck her tits hard and blow a huge load all over her. She's got it in her hair and everything. Poor little virgin did not know who the fuck she was playing with here. This girl is a happy camper. But, of course, we had already agreed to just be friends, so I go to sleep and next morning she's asking if I will call...."Do you call your friends?"

I ended up calling her about a week later, and we embarked on an amazing sexual journey. It took another six months or so before we finally went all the way, but it was not much of a   problem, actually. We ended up doing all sorts of nasty things. Public sex, videotape, screaming orgasms, dirty talk....you name it.

I often wonder what it was about her that made her so amazing in bed.

Perhaps, she was just born with an amazing talent and an amazing body.

Or maybe it was something more. Maybe it was the magnitude of her conflict. She wanted so badly to be good. Yet, the urge to be bad was even stronger.

Brad P

davidshadelikes.com/brad

SECTION 5

NEXT STEPS TO BEING A MASTERFUL LOVER

WHERE TO LEARN MORE

The next step that you want to take is to study my program "Give Women Wild Screaming Orgasms." This includes the correct knowledge and beliefs to being a Masterful Lover, sexual techniques for giving women incredible pleasure, being comfortable with her sexuality, and developing the enabling beliefs for sexual confidence.

It also includes my audio CDs, in which I tell you how to use sexy, dirty talk to drive her wild with excitement; "The Art of Sexy Dirty Talk." It also comes with a bonus CD in which I tell you "one step at a time" how you can use a woman's fantasies to lead her to become a ruthlessly expressive sexual being; "How To Set The Foundation For A Wild Sexual Relationship."

WildScreamingOrgasms.com

Napolean Hill wrote in "*Think and Grow Rich*" that the most important decision you will ever make is selection of a wife. Success begins by choosing wisely. If you select the wrong woman, you will be forever frustrated. If you select the correct woman, you will live a life of love and hot passionate sex. You will discover what to look for in a woman that will make for a successful relationship, and exactly how to do that quickly and easily, in my program "Select Women Wisely".

SelectWomenWisely.com

My secret weapon is phone sex. If you want to actually hear David Shade talking dirty, you can hear it in "Give Women Hot Phone Sex," which includes three audio CDs of actual recorded phone sex episodes, where you will hear me talking very dirty, and hear the actual female screaming orgasms that result. You will discover, by example, exactly how you can make your woman come with just the sound of your voice, and keep her coming for as long as you like!

GiveWomenHotPhoneSex.com

Finally, "Advanced Sexual Hypnosis," hypnosis for couples. This is the really advanced, far out stuff for using NLP, hypnosis, and energy for giving women indescribable pleasure.

AdvancedSexualHypnosis.com

In review: Start out with "Give Women Wild Screaming Orgasms." Get good at the sexual techniques and develop your sexual confidence. Then, study the audio CDs and become good at using sexy dirty talk. Then move to "Give Women Hot Phone Sex" to totally open herself to you sexually. Then get into the really advanced stuff with the "Manual."

For further reading, check out my articles on my blog at:

DavidShadesBlog.com

All this and more can be found at my web site for developing yourself into a personally and sensually powerful man.

RenegadeSexExpert.com

I also include the list of books and mentors that have affected me along the way. I have consumed countless books and resources on this topic and can recommend the few that contributed leading work.

"Dangerous Men and Adventurous Women" Edited by Jayne Ann Krentz, University of Pennsylvania Press, 1992. Mark Cunningham suggests we read this. It is a collection of essays by 19 leading romance authors on the appeal of the romance novel. Describes all the traits of the romantic hero.

"A Passion For More" by Susan Shapiro Barash, Berkeley Hills Books, 2001. The stories of 57 women and what drove them to have extramarital affairs. In almost every case, the woman's

thoughts are consumed by the man with whom she has the exciting sex.

"*Private Thoughts*" by Wendy Maltz & Suzie Boss, New World Library, 2001. This book presents an outstanding thesis on the why and how of female fantasies.

"*Story of O*" by Pauline Reage, Running Press, 1954. It is a true story written by a woman under a pseudonym, but whose identity was revealed in 1994 as Dominique Aury. Considered the classic reference for BDSM.

"*9 1/2 Weeks A Memoir of a Love Affair*" by Elizabeth McNeill, Harper Perennial, 1978. It is a true story also written by a woman under a pseudonym, but whose identity has never been revealed.

"*Different Loving: The World of Sexual Dominance and Submission*" by Gloria G. Brame, Jon Jacobs, Will Brame, Villard Books, 1996. A good introductory guide book into BDSM.

"*My Secret Garden*" by Nancy Friday, Pocket Books, 1973. Friday interviewed hundreds of women and documented in intricate detail all the fantasies. It is fascinating and very eye opening.

"*The Hite Report*" by Shere Hite, McMillan Publishing, 1976. A huge study of female sexuality. Read how sexually frustrated women truly are.

"*The Six Pillars of Self-Esteem*" by Nathaniel Branden, Bantam Books, 1994. The recognized definition of self-esteem.

"*Think and Grow Rich*" by Napoleon Hill, Wilder Publications, 1960. The greatest book ever written. Hill worked with and studied the great captains of industry, such as Carnegie, Edison, and Ford, and documented all the steps to success. His book is to billionaires what Machiavelli's "The Prince" was to kings. Apply the teachings of this book toward female sexuality and truly anything is possible.

GET YOUR FREE CD TODAY!

Receive a FREE CD in the mail!
In this one hour interview, David Shade
reveals to you the secrets of...

How To Keep The Relationship Exciting!

For details and to receive your Free CD,
go to my website:
RenegadeSexExpert.com

FREE VIP INNER CIRCLE OFFER

Special FREE Gift from the Author

Test Drive David Shade's
VIP Inner Circle Membership
for 39 days **FREE**

VIP Inner Circle Newsletter
Exclusive Audio Interviews

Get Your FREE Gift Here:
Masterful-Lover-VIP.com

There is a small, one-time charge to cover postage for the free VIP Inner Circle Membership, and you have no obligation to continue at the low monthly rate. In fact, should you continue with membership, you can later cancel at any time.

FREE STUFF LINKED TO THIS BOOK

To help you get full value from this book,
there is a collection of
FREE EXTRA RESOURCES
waiting for you at
RenegadeSexExpert.com

FREE e-mail course "Secrets to Mind Blowing Sex!"

FREE teleseminar with David Shade

FREE access to ask David Shade your
most burning question

Printed in the USA
CPSIA information can be obtained
at www.ICGtesting.com
LVHW041437250124
769628LV00012B/231

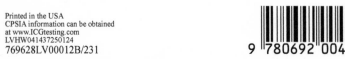